Four Wheel Alignment for Your Life:
The Model.

by Dmitry Kondratyev

Visit Dmitry Kondratyev at
positivecoachingllc.com

#4WA4YL

Stephanie Bolton, JD, Editor
Uros Dedovic, Illustrator
Kristin Hope, Editor and Cover Design

Accolades and Testimonials

"Dmitry blends organizational behavior and organizational psychology theory with life coaching and relevant research. He presents information and his own coaching model in an easy to digest way, leaving you with food for thought, 'aha' moments, and actionable items."
Maria Paredes. *Organizational Psychologist and Certified Professional Coach. Great Britain.*

"I have been privileged to witness Dmitry's coaching. His coaching demeanor is very skillful. He will get out of his comfort zone to lure you out of yours. As a coach, he walks the talk - an asset demonstrating his leadership skills. Dmitry sees the wisdom in you and believes in your abilities and values. With his authentic presence he guides you towards insights and supports you through obstacles. Dmitry has what it takes to give you the much needed push in moving forward towards a much better self. I highly recommend Dmitry for anyone who needs to find clarity and motivation. Dmitry will inspire you and leverage your strengths with his powerful questions and non-judgmental stance."
Marika Gillis. *Trainer, Mentor, and Certified Professional Coach. Hong Kong.*

"Dmitry has done a masterful job of creating a unique way to look at life. The illustrations and figures included in the chapters are great visuals, and the powerful coaching questions encourage readers to take a deeper introspective look at what might be out of alignment. Readers are left with the challenge to pursue a more balanced life for a smoother ride that leads to a meaningful destination."
Mary Selzer. *Professional Certified Coach. Board member and past-president of International Coach Federation, Michigan Chapter. ICF mentor / coach. Speaker and published author. USA.*

"Powerful principles that challenge you to ask the tough questions, then motivate you to act!"
Heather L Celerin. *Founder and President. Celerin Consulting Services. USA.*

"Coaching with Dmitry is a life exploring experience and good moments to reflect and acquire insightful strategies to move forward. Each coaching session helped me to create a new vision with appropriate tools & strategies to put into action. I had a space to explore and discover new perspectives, insights and tools to achieve my goals in life, career, and business. Thank you Dmitry for your strong and wonderful support. I appreciate my journey with you and I am grateful to have you as my fantastic coach."
Areeya M. *Thailand.*

"Dmitry Kondratyev has been my coach for over a year and has been a valuable part of my business. He is focused on understanding my goals and needs and in helping me achieve them. Dmitry is as capable of maneuvering through strategic discussions as he is in advising and assisting with some very tactical issues. I too am a business coach and appreciate his approach and methods."
Charlie Puissegur. *Owner. CHPuissegur & Associates. USA.*

"Dmitry is a highly skilled coach and a reliable accountability partner. Thanks to his support I met all my goals during a personal 100-day challenge. His ability to paraphrase and support visualization through the use of metaphors is unique. Always on time and positive, he is the perfect partner for a successful coaching journey!"
Rossella Pin. *Coach Mentor. CPC, PCC, EIA Senior Practitioner. Trainer & Italian Programme Director at International Coach Academy. Italy.*

"As a returning client, I wholeheartedly recommend Dmitry as a highly skilled, insightful and dedicated coach. We started working together over a year ago on a business venture that I wanted to be part of. After experiencing tremendous results, I decided to return to Dmitry to tackle other professional goals and to experience similar success. I am very grateful for his dedication to the field and to the client experience."
Ashley Gork. *Account Executive. Strategic Partner. Certified Life Coach. USA.*

Table of Contents

Acknowledgements

The idea to write this book came from influences and wisdoms bestowed upon me by instructors of the International Coach Academy. Countless hours spent discussing, coaching, and being coached have somehow connected what I already knew in a new way. My deepest gratitude goes to all the instructors and classmates.

The support of my family was essential. My special thanks to my wife Olga who endured countless hours in the company of a mumbling husband. Jacob, my ten-year-old son, remained my biggest fan throughout the entire project. His confidence in me, at times, was greater than my own. The rest of my family remained fairly curious of when I would cross the finish line. That kept me going strong. Thank you!

I also want to thank my colleagues at Main Street Bank. Some provided validation of my ideas. Conversations with others helped to shape certain perspectives that found their way in this book. Thank you!

Another special thanks goes to my editor Stephanie Bolton for her words of encouragement and professionalism. Another special thanks to Kristin Hope, editor, for helping me to cross the finish line and for a brilliant cover design. Uros Dedovic, is not only a gifted illustrator, but, I suspect might be a mind reader. Residing seven times zones away he, somehow, always knows what style I am looking for!

My warmest thanks goes to Ike Engelbaum of Michigan Entrepreneur Network. Ike provided me with countless opportunities to come to his radio show and talk about life, coaching, and the Model. His unwavering optimism is a rare find.

Introduction

Every working day we follow a certain routine and for many it includes driving to and from work. We drive to the grocery store, to socialize, and to visit our relatives. We drive to and from vacation destinations. We drive a lot!

Every year we share the road with more drivers than the year before. Traffic does not get lighter and bad driving is something we often discuss at work around the watercooler. Someone got cut off, someone got the finger, and someone else got sucked into a bout of road rage. On and on we go. Before we realize our audience loses interest in our story because there is nothing new to be learned from the experiences that we have already had.

Once in a while, you will be the only one on the road. It may be an early morning or late at night, or you may find yourself off the beaten path with no other vehicles in sight. Enjoying the view, you adjust your seat to a more comfortable position as if you are about to watch a movie. As your whole body relaxes, you loosen your grip on the steering wheel.

All of a sudden you notice that you are not traveling in a straight line and it takes a constant effort to keep things straight. This may be a bit annoying and you may realize for the first time that's how you have always been driving. You may have never noticed this before because you have been busy keeping an eye on traffic and trying to anticipate the behaviors of other drivers.

This constant need to adjust your steering wheel to keep traveling straight is caused by the wheels being out of alignment. Whether you know what "wheel alignment" is or not is irrelevant. You stand to gain a whole lot by learning what it means metaphorically, as this book is not about cars, trucks, or RVs. This book is about life so keep on reading.

Read this book from start to finish. The concepts that are built in Chapter One: The Model are used in the chapter that follows. Keep in mind car terminology is just a metaphor.

Business jargon is full of car references like "we'll park that," "brand alignment," "to throw someone under the bus," and "spinning the wheels." Words like *drive, spark, gear, brakes,* and *shifting* are every-day office jargon. These phrases and words, like tiny dots, have been out there all along. The Model connects them in a powerful way that is easy to remember.

As you read the first chapter, keep in mind that simplicity of The Model is by design. Our brains overcomplicate things that we already know. The unprecedented ease of access to information, often wrong and confusing, does not help to learn or to retain the fundamentals. In our case, we will be covering the fundamentals of a mechanism that drives much of our life experiences.

Chapter One: The Model.

The Four Wheel Alignment Model.

This all started when I was studying at the International Coach Academy. All the students had an assignment to come up with a coaching model. As a life-long car enthusiast, and a former Master Certified Automotive Technician, I couldn't help but see a car analogy in many aspects of my corporate life. The life coaching model that is based on a car analogy came to me naturally. Please refer to Figure 1.1. The focus of this chapter is the Model and the Four Wheels. The rest of the book will discuss the relationships between the Four Wheels.

Fig. 1.1

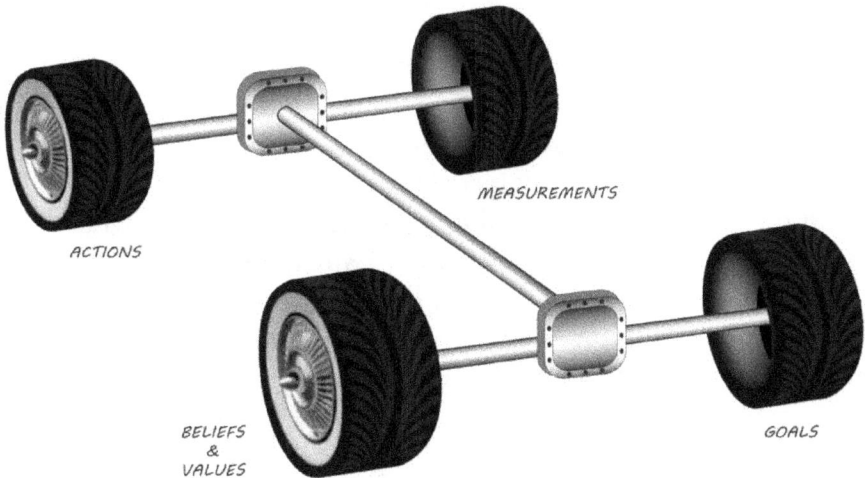

ACTIONS

MEASUREMENTS

BELIEFS
&
VALUES

GOALS

Wheel One – Beliefs and Values

Wheel Two – Goals

Wheel Three – Actions

Wheel Four – Measurements

Wheel One: Beliefs and Values.

Throughout this book, I will refer to Wheel One as either the Belief Wheel or the Value Wheel depending on the context. First, we will examine the Big Three questions about the Belief Wheel:

1. What are our Beliefs?

2. What purpose do our Beliefs serve?

3. What causes our Beliefs to change?

1

Our Beliefs are like a computer program. The program scans the territories near and far and asks some simple true or false questions. Depending on the answers, we ascertain the terrain for safety and various opportunities to strive. For example, looking at a never before seen object, the program may ask "This looks like something I already know: true or false?" If the answer is "true," the question that follows is "What I already know is safe: true or false?" If the answer is "false," the new object will be filed under the label "dangerous" and we would try to avoid it.

Dozens of "true or false" questions are asked every minute of every hour. We do not always cognitively register these questions. Often, when someone asks us what we are thinking about, we reply "nothing." This can either mean that we do not want to share our thoughts or we cannot put many pieces of the puzzle together to form a coherent story. It has been estimated that in a 24-hour period we have 50,000 – 70,000 thoughts while the number of words we utter fluctuates between 7,000 – 21,000 for the same time period. Why such a disparity?

We use speech for a variety of reasons. We communicate information; give out orders; tell true stories and lies; and share thoughts, feelings, and emotions. While we are busy communicating, the true or false program is multitasking and scanning the reactions to the words we say. Speech requires a lot of computing power. Therefore, when someone asks us, "What are you thinking about?" it is easier to just say "nothing" than try to explain what we are actually thinking in the moment. Some try. They use words like *kinda, sort of,* and *like,* to explain the unexplainable. They might as well say "nothing."

The better question to ask is what you suspect or fear the person is thinking about. You may already have an idea. This is why you were curious in the first place, isn't it? If you can conjure up enough courage to ask a specific question, "nothing" will not be the answer. The Beliefs of the person answering your question will run their own true or false program and will optimize the answer accordingly. As a result, the most self-serving content will fill the air.

Our Beliefs are also tiny files, each describing the smallest possible attributes of a reality. The best examples of that are the works of the nuclear physicists. Recent discoveries in the fields of condensed matter physics like nanotechnology, which deals with files as tiny as an atom, have shaped beliefs for those involved in the field directly, as well as those who are involved in applying nanotechnology. For nanotechnology scientists, the ability to control matters and processes at the molecular levels is an everyday reality, a confident true in their Beliefs. Medical, pharmaceutical, cosmetics, and water treatment industries would not embrace nanotechnology if they did not believe it was a scientifically sound and a technologically possible reality.

The Beliefs do not have to be supported by science in order for people to embrace them. Religious beliefs are good examples of Beliefs that people hold even though these Beliefs may not be supported by science. For instance, believing that God is the ultimate power and his presence can be found everywhere is sufficient to explain how the world works. At the same time, science does not seem to have as many universal answers compared to religion. Science is less holistic and has separate subjects for various matters and processes. Even though there are only seven basic branches of science, the number of "ologies," or fields of scientific studies, is approaching a thousand. Compare that number to the small handful of major religions.

Each true or false question, when asked, sounds simple. The complexity comes from the fact that most of the time there is no right or wrong answer. What we have learned in school by getting most of the true or false questions correct on tests has very little value when it comes to life, career, or business choices. The ever-changing landscape of reality feels like going to the next level of a computer game where the requirements are getting tougher. Beliefs act as a foundation that enables other processes necessary for success.

2

Our Beliefs serve a purpose that is similar to parents when they are asked "Why?" by their children. We formed our first set of Beliefs once our parents answered enough of our own "Why?" questions. From that moment we realized the power that comes from knowing how things work. The ability to answer our own "why?" and "true or false" gives us a great deal of autonomy.

When it comes to explaining the way we are, as opposed to

the way the world is, we are forced to turn the magnifying glass on ourselves. Our Beliefs reveal the reasons behind our thoughts, feelings, and actions. The reason to have Beliefs is to be able to explain ourselves to ourselves and to others.

As we progressed through our childhood and adolescence, our Beliefs have constantly added new pieces of information coming primarily from our family, friends, daycare, kindergarten, and school. By the time we are ready to enter life as young adults, our Beliefs have guided us through a relatively simple and predictable environment. The rough period some experience as teenagers is over. By the time we are in our early twenties, we believe that we know all that there is to know. As we get our first real job, get married, and drive off into an independent life our Beliefs will soon be challenged.

3

So far I've touched on two kinds of Beliefs. This first kind was based on scientific support and the second was based on religion. Any changes in our factual or religious knowledge or experience are likely to cause changes in our Beliefs. There are other factors that affect our Beliefs.

As we get our career going, we get exposed to some strong influences that come from our immediate supervisors. Do you remember your first performance review? Did you have to change a few things about yourself as the result of it? If the answer is yes, your Beliefs about your ability to perform, or even about your self-worth have been changed by authority. To some degree, college professors, athletic coaches, and high school teachers may play similar roles of authority; however, bad grades will not get you evicted and your car repossessed, but losing a job might.

In an attempt to adapt and do well, we seek a friendship with co-workers. They are a wealth of information when it comes to unwritten rules, shortcuts, and your supervisor's preferences. This information will be shared generously once you are accepted into the group of co-workers. One of the ways this acceptance is gained is by exhibiting behavior similar to the behavior of the group. Again, this may resemble a high school or college clique; the difference is that your job is now at stake. In looking for stronger bonds we might allow our Beliefs to take on different answers to some true or false questions. This shared part of our Beliefs is called Group Beliefs.

After a period of time on a new job, usually 12-18 months, a set of new individual Beliefs will be added and tested.

When we get married and enter a new circle of family and friends, a similar process occurs. Constant feedback replaces a less frequent performance review and the support of certain family members or new friends is just as crucial. The stakes are just as high, if not higher, for the family dynamics are usually in the center of our personal lives. They influence us even when we are at work.

As atoms form molecules, our Beliefs form our Values. People of various backgrounds may share similar Values. Figure 1.2 is a list of some of the most common Values. Which 5 or 10 would you say are your core Values?

Fig. 1.2

Authenticity	Achievement	Adventure	Authority	Autonomy
Balance	Beauty	Boldness	Compassion	Challenge
Citizenship	Community	Competency	Contribution	Creativity
Curiosity	Determination	Fairness	Faith	Fame
Friendship	Fun	Growth	Happiness	Honesty
Humor	Influence	Harmony	Justice	Kindness
Knowledge	Leadership	Learning	Love	Loyalty
Openness	Optimism	Peace	Pleasure	Poise
Popularity	Purpose	Recognition	Religion	Reputation
Respect	Responsibility	Security	Self Respect	Service
Spirituality	Stability	Success	Status	Trust
Vision	Wealth	Well-Being	Wisdom	Zen

Wheel Two: Goals.

Most of our deliberate actions are like driving a car. We reach our destination by a constant process of pointing the front wheels in the specific direction we want to go. Bad weather, potholes, traffic, and construction are all obstacles in our way. They cause us to change lanes or take alternate routes until we reach the final destination. We call this course-correction. Many of the actions in life are also caused by constant course-correction. Setbacks of various kinds are inevitable and a push-through strategy does not always work. For instance, if we are sick and need medical attention, some of our projects will have to wait until we get better.

Our Goals may not be obvious to an on-looker: from a distance we all look like busy bees. Nevertheless, our Goals must be very clear to us if we want to take ownership of our lives.

Most of the motivational speaking regarding goal setting is quite predictable as most will talk about setting big, extraordinary long-term goals, like becoming a millionaire or competing in the Olympics. Imagining reaching seemingly unattainable goals makes people feel good at the moment but does not motivate them for more than a day.

There are several ways to think about Goals. For instance, below are some other words that are used in a similar way:

- Achievement

- Destination

- Dream

- Mission

- Result

- Vision

We turn our attention to the field of psychology. The desire to explain human behavior in a systematic way and to come up with theories that will predict human behavior has been one of the Goals, no pun intended, of many prominent psychologists.

Modern psychology is a relatively new field. It is only about 130 years old, as compared to math or astronomy which dates back thousands of years. At first, the focus of psychology was to treat or cure mentally ill individuals. They presented opportunities to study abnormalities and create new methodologies to improve the lives of those who were considered "not normal." World War I and World War II produced an unprecedented amount of cases of mental illness because of the traumatic experiences of war. This kept the psychologists occupied for the first part of the 20th Century.

With the rise of computer science and the first talks about artificial intelligence, psychologists were called to help model the human psyche in a way that can be programmed. Starting in the 1950s, generous funding from government and large corporate sectors kept scientists busy with trials and errors. The fact that many attempts to map out and to code the human brain ended up in failure, proved, indirectly, its complexity.

Finally, by the late 1990s, psychologists started to pay attention to mentally healthy individuals and to see what some of the traits exhibited by those that were able to move up the socioeconomic ladder looked like. For the first time, striving individuals and communities were formally studied using scientific methodologies of systematic observations, measurements, and experiments. The findings pointed out the fact that the self-preservation "code" embedded in the brain was responsible for conserving energy often overrides energy - consuming actions motivational speakers are calling for.

At the same time as a group of experts from different fields were trying to create artificial intelligence, a group of experts studying organizational behavior brought forth the importance of having a system of goals and incentives at various levels of corporate management. The idea of fiscal budgeting was hardly a new concept in the 1960s or 1970s, but the introduction of a psychological approach to goal setting was. A new type of management that would introduce terms like *mission, vision,* and *strategy* needed new tools to engage employees of all levels in more productive activities that are measurable, and to tie the results to monetary incentives. By the 1980s, organizational culture became a field of study in its own right.

One of the most widely known and accepted criteria for goal setting is S.M.A.R.T. The abbreviation first appeared in 1981 in a business publication and was based on the works of organizational behavior and management theorists of the preceding decades.[1] Figure 1.3 explains the SMART criteria in several terms. First, it explains what each letter means. Second, it shows what problems can be solved by lining up each letter with a question. By answering all the questions and keeping bolded words for later reference, we would have a structure that would help us reach our SMART goals.

Fig. 1.3

Letter	Meaning	Question
S	Specific	**What** is the Goal?
M	Measurable	**How much / How many?**
A	Assignable	Who will works the Goal?
R	Realistic	Is the Goal realistic?
T	Time-Bound	**When** the Goal be achieved?

There are other variations of SMART that were later added to the list, but they have not changed the essence of the original. SMART is a powerful approach to set goals and to run companies of any size. SMART criteria has stood the test of time, as it helped bridge the gap between corporate and personal interests.

I am no stranger to SMART: I have spent over two decades in the corporate world. I have been asked many "What? How many? By When?" questions. By looking at Figure 1.3 we can cross-reference these questions to the letters "S," "M," and "T." There was no need for "A" as the goals were assigned to me, and whether or not these goals were "R" for realistic was not up for debate.

After years of achieving SMART goals, receiving raises and being promoted, some recurring themes have emerged. Goals would always go up year after year. Upward movement through corporate ranks does not exempt one from having performance goals. Even Presidents or CEOs have to answer to a Board of Directors. In turn, the Board, among other things, is responsible for maintaining and increasing the value of the company's stock. Authority power peaks at the Board of Directors level and goes out to shareholders. If you own stock in the company you are employed by, the power comes full circle, as the Board Members are voted in by the shareholders.

There is one problem. SMART criteria offers very little when it comes to personal Goals. After all, people are not companies and their Goals are not always monetary. As an exercise, I wrote my own SMART criteria for setting personal Goals. Using the same approach as in Figure 1.3, Figure 1.4 offers a different set of meanings and questions.

Fig. 1.4

Letter	Meaning	Question
S	Stretchable	Will the Goal help me learn and grow?
M	Memorable	[How] Will I remember what the Goal is?
A	Aligned	Why am I pursuing the Goal?
R	Resourced	Am I willing to commit resources?
T	Taskable	How will I achieve my Goal?

As the world around us changes constantly, we are in a life-long journey of learning. We can choose to react to changes, or we can choose to proactively set Goals that will give us opportunities to learn and grow with changes. The word *stretchable* comes from a visual where a stack of paper is held together by a rubber band. Each new piece of paper represents a new piece of knowledge. Therefore, the rubber band would have to stretch a little each time a new piece of paper is added to the stack.

There is something good to be said about visual boards, white boards, journals, and planners. They help us create Goals and hold them in our point of view. The twenty dollars I invested in a dry erase board is yielding the highest rate of return compared to other investments I have made! Goals I write on the board are always there as a reminder as I pass to and from my bedroom. The board reminds me about my Goals in the morning and before I go to bed. This simple set-up keeps me focused on my highest level Goals. What system do you use?

Whose goals are driving most of our actions? At work, it is usually the goals of your employer or customers. After all, this is how you make a living. Because money helps us in many aspects of our lives, work goals tend to have a strong influence, and compete with the time needed to accomplish personal goals. This competition is sometimes referred to as work-life balance.

Speaking of influence, TV and Internet advertisements are like the smartest person in the room. The person knows what we should buy and why. TV and Internet advertisements can convince us to make a purchase by using reasoning or emotional appeal by making us feel like part of a group we are looking up to. For instance, car or beer commercials target certain audiences in such a way that after watching the commercials the audience would have all the reasons to make the purchase! These reasons are often far from rational, though they may appear as such. "Do you know what time it is? It's Miller Time!" is an example of a powerful advertisement that uses time as a reason for purchase and consumption.

Occasionally, it may seem that work goals and mass media influences run the majority of our lives. It seems that way because many times we let them. The only way to reclaim your ownership is to intentionally align your Goals to your higher Values and Beliefs. This is why "A" stands for aligned. When our Goals come from our Values and Beliefs, we become more authentic and true to ourselves.

Time is a finite "R" for resource. Regardless of who we are, 24 hours in a day is all we have. How we spend our time largely determines who we are. If we decide to take on a new goal, we simply must make the time for actions necessary to achieve it. Same goes for financial commitment. Not all of our Goals will be achieved. Factors outside of our control may present challenges that will be a higher priority. Therefore, we may have to let go of money, and let go of efforts we put in. Willingness to commit the necessary resources, as well as accept the risk, is a must.

The last letter is "T" for taskable. Our Goals must be complex enough to contain more than one task, but not so complex that we cannot break it into doable tasks. For example, if the Goal is to be happy and it requires a seven figure bank account balance, we might not even know where to start. Time and money may be wasted chasing that Goal. The ambiguity of the Goal will not make it SMART. On the other hand, in a pursuit of happiness, smoking a joint or drinking a shot may sound like a viable, single-task proposition. However, the simplicity of execution, not to mention health risks, may not make this Goal SMART either.

To summarize, the original SMART criteria is a valuable tool to manage production and sales. It answers three principle questions: "What?," "How Many?," and "When?" These questions can be applied to a range of activities, from lemonade stands and Girl Scout cookie sales, to car and truck production and sales. In most companies, we can find an area where constant activity is aimed to grow a customer base either directly or to support such activity. Additionally, we can find areas of quality control and risk management. Their goals are to reduce the number of defects and exceptions.

Alternatively, SMART for personal Goals answers "What?," "Why?," and "How?" questions. Be warned: coming up with a goal that is not somehow influenced by the work environment, or has not been already mentioned by the advertisers, may seem hard. It is. The way to make personal Goals truly personal is to connect them to our Beliefs and Values by answering the "Why" question. This is the way to align the first two Wheels of the Model.

Wheel Three: Actions.

We are constantly active. Actions may be visible or invisible. Invisible Actions include thinking as well as experiencing feelings and emotions. Have you ever taken a nice, peaceful walk in a park on a Sunday morning, daydreaming about the day ahead, and feeling unsettled at the same time? To others the only visible part was you, physically walking, one foot in front of the other.

Actions can also be of maintenance, learning, and play. Taking daily showers, preparing meals, and going through a work routine are all examples of maintenance Actions. There are situations at work that present learning Action opportunities. In the work environment these learning Actions are often masked as problems. Thus, we tend to avoid them. Finally, our hobbies are examples of play Actions and they often reside at the bottom of our priority list.

Skills that we have learned are the examples of exercising control over our Actions. Looking at the performances of professional speakers, musicians, and dancers, we do not see all the hours of hard work that went into achieving the mastery of their craft. Instead, we see smiling, relaxed faces that communicate happiness and joy. At that moment, we are fooled into believing that what they do comes easy. This is how the magic is created. The magic of speaking can transform impossible ideas into possibilities.

Visible Actions are relatively easier to control compared to our thoughts. I believe that it is even harder to control our feelings and emotions. Figure 1.5 gives a visual to the notion of relative control. We will talk more about feelings and emotions in Chapter Eight.

Fig. 1.5

Control		
Easier	Harder	Very Hard
Visible Physical Actions		
Observable Behaviors	Invisible Actions	
	Thoughts	Feelings and Emotions

Actions, visible or not, do not occur in sequence such as maintenance, learning, and play. For example, if we sing while we take a shower, we are combining maintenance and play. While at work, by going through a similar routine of combining various types of Actions, we may come up with a faster way to handle similar tasks.

It is important to acknowledge that we live in constant interaction with the society that has rules as to what Actions are acceptable or not. This adds another layer of complexity in predicting our Actions by establishing cause and effect between the invisible and visible in various environments. The complexity of Actions has been studied by sociologists, psychologists, and many other professionals.

Psychology uses the term *behavior* to describe the range of human Actions. If you are familiar with the terminology, let's agree that for the purpose of the Four Wheel Alignment Model, both Actions and behaviors are the same. This simplification will allow for a better flow and will possibly save a few trees.

Actions, the third Wheel of the Model, is the doer that moves things from dreams to achievements. It is the replicator from *Star Trek* that materializes objects into existence. That said, with larger or less intangible Goals, the finishing line may not be obvious. This necessitates a system that will tell us where we are relative to where we were, similar to the GPS system employed by your vehicle or smart-phone.

Wheel Four: Measurements.

Our physical, three-dimensional world knows many units of measuring distance, weight, volume, speed, time, and other properties of objects, substances, and agents. Our human world added the ways to measure the results of human Actions towards achieving Values listed in Figure 1.2. The issue with such Measurements is that there are no known standards when it comes to Values. Unlike a metric ton, which is 1,000 kilograms or 2,205 pounds, there is no such thing as a metric ton of happiness or love.

For two millennia, the philosophers in their pursuit of wisdom, have studied questions of values, knowledge, reason, and mind. The philosophers are often criticized for not providing the easy answers to the questions they have been asking for a long period of time. Lack of easy answers evidences the complexity of the questions. In turn, this translates in acknowledgement of the complexity of human nature.

Advances in science have made our biological lives longer and safer. Advances in technology have made communication and access to information easier than ever. Why then do we get more questions every time we progress? If progress was defined as a practical application of a solved question or problem, wouldn't we have to admit that humanity failed because we created more problems along the way?

To simplify and standardize the way we think, political, legal, economic, cultural, and educational systems tell us what answers are right and what answers are wrong. Policy makers within each system do all the hard thinking for us. All we have to do is to follow. Acceptance became a reward for getting most of the answers right and aligning our Actions accordingly. Isolation became a punishment for getting the answers wrong and acting differently.

Coming up with a scale of the continuums of right to wrong, rich to poor, happy to unhappy, truth to lie, and so forth, the comparative approach took roots due to its uncomplicated nature.

Comparing ourselves to others is a continuation of a grade school "compare and contrast" exercise. We were taught to look for similarities and differences in a systematic manner and were graded on our abilities to do so. By the time we enter the Life of employment, apply for our first credit card, and pay our own rent, we have compared our parents, relatives, and friends to many other people. We have established our own benchmarks for things we consider important in life, like how much money one makes or how serious one's relationship is. Inferring wealth and status from the size and location of one's house, type of car, or brand of clothing has been mastered. Now, the race is on to outdo friends from high school and college.

High school reunions could be looked at as an exhibition of materialistic achievements. By the time the ten year reunion rolls around, the awards would go to those who got married first, who had their first child, who makes the most money, and who drives the most expensive car. By the twenty year reunion, things are quite different. Some get divorced, some lose their jobs and businesses, while those who lagged behind are now getting ahead. The race is no longer fun and the prior successes are now the source of disappointments and resentment. Comparing ourselves to others is no longer helpful.

The alternative to comparing ourselves to others is to take a periodic inventory of the things we have at that moment in our lives and be thankful for them. This is called gratitude. Practicing gratitude leads to an appreciation of what we already have as well as what is new that has come into our lives. The more things and people we learn to appreciate, the more fulfilled we feel.

The practice of gratitude, as great as it is to keep a level head during the good times and help us during tough times, is no substitute for intentional Actions towards Goals that are in alignment with our Beliefs. Measuring our own progress requires a new type of thinking. Consider these:

- Comparing yourself to others is inevitable. In doing so, don't get down on yourself. Instead, when you think about other people, try to empathize with their problems rather than focusing on what they have that you don't.

- The more famous and powerful people you get to know by reading their biographies, for example, the more you will know and understand the true price of wealth, fame, and power. Are you willing to pay the price?

- Accepting the fact that it is physically impossible for a mentally healthy individual to be constantly happy and enjoying life on an emotional level is the first step in a two-step process. The second step is to force negative thoughts out and intentionally replace them with positive thoughts. For example, by changing "I hate when it is hot outside" to "I love sunny weather, since winters in Michigan are nothing but gray skies," I would psych myself up to enjoy the outdoor activities, especially when staying inside is not an option.

- Life allows for many definitions of my Values. Whatever definition I choose is the right definition for me at that moment. I accept full responsibility for all the future successes and failures in trying to live by my Values. Keep in mind, Values are subject to change without prior notice.

Once our thinking becomes more holistic, more positive, and more flexible, we will start to look at our own Life with greater care and empathy. We will start measuring our Life in terms of how much closer we are getting to living the Life of our Values. Things that surround us do not define us, they are mere articles of choice made at a point in time that reflect the Values we had then.

When it comes to a formal methodology of measuring intangible aspects of our Lives, psychologists and sociologists rely primarily on questionnaires. Sample size or the number of people filling out questionnaires is very important. The larger the sample size, the more accurate the data. In turn, the more accurate the data, the more reliable the conclusion of the study is. This logic seems straightforward and in line with the rules of statistics. However, the questionnaire itself is not the same as a ruler or a scale.

Questionnaires rely on our own assessments use questions that often start with "on the scale of 1 to 10..." One of the better-known tests is the Wheel of Life. It asks the participants to rate their level of satisfaction in eight areas of their lives. See Figure 1.6.

Fig. 1.6

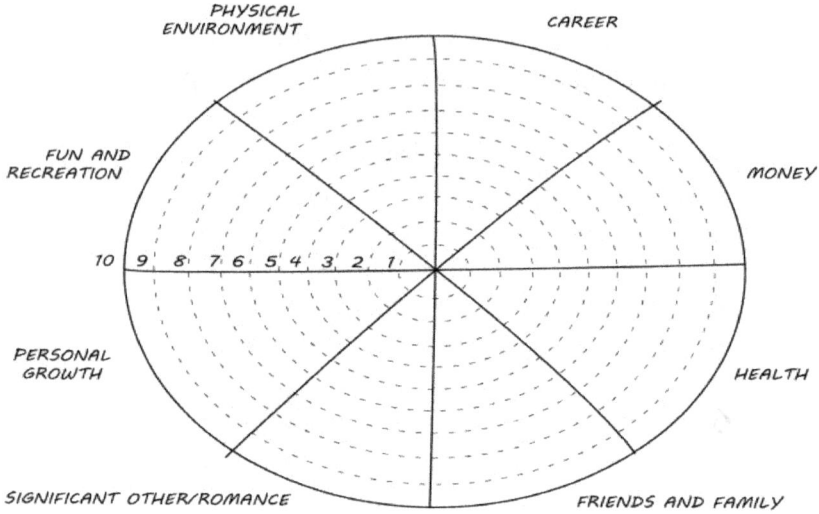

Once filled out, it may look like Figure 1.7.

Fig. 1.7

EXAMPLE

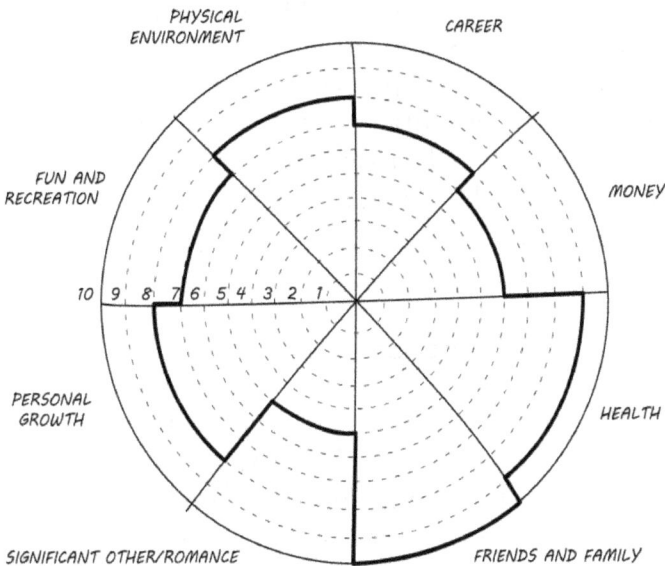

I took this test three times in one week: the first time was on Wednesday afternoon, the second time on a Friday night, and the third on a Sunday morning. In total, my rating changed in all eight areas by one or two points! This was surprising since people that know me well would likely consider me to be a bit rigid or stubborn. If that was true, why would I change my own perception of my own life?

Once more I was reminded that timing, if not everything, is very important. We think slightly differently about the same things based on our physical and emotional state. Spending Sunday morning in a park with my family boosted my own rating in the Family and Friends as well as Physical Environment areas.

This simple exercise provides a great insight on the value of questionnaires based on self-ranking. They are important, however, the ever-changing environment that surrounds us influences our emotional, physical, and mental states. As a result, the "rulers and scales" are constantly changing. Awareness of this fact and acceptance of "drifting" self-assessments should not discourage us from keeping on course towards Values that serve as beacons. As I am writing this, I can't help but hear in my head what I consider great advice that comes from Dory, a family movie character: "Just keep swimming!" Indeed, it is time to wrap-up this chapter.

Chapter Summary.

The Four Wheel Alignment Model consists of the Four Wheels: Beliefs and Values, Goals, Actions, and Measurements. As we form as individuals during childhood, school years, and college, all the wheels, due to hard interactions with new environments of life, often get out of alignment. As we enter our adult life, the rubber meets the road and our independent choices are put to the test.

The test of life never stops, but it does get harder and can cause the Wheels to get out of alignment. A great deal of effort is required to maintain a forward-facing position with a positive outlook. By learning how to think in a more holistic manner and consciously changing perspective from negative to positive, we will start acquiring the self-control necessary to navigate an ever changing reality.

In the chapters to come, we will examine the relationships between the Wheels and cover topics relating to the alignment between Beliefs and Values, Goals, Actions, and Measurements.

Chapter Two: Relationship Between the Beliefs and Values Wheel, and the Goals Wheel.

Significance.

In this chapter, we will examine the relationship between the Beliefs and Values Wheel and the Goals Wheel. Many times we stop pursuing our Goals because we can no longer see value in reaching them. In that case, Goals lose their significance.

Sometimes, we get discouraged by others. There might be a situation where any further pursuit of a goal may jeopardize our relationships. Many Beliefs come into play that will influence our decisions. As a result, Goals may be abandoned or postponed until sometime in the future, when they regain their significance.

Values in a workplace comprise what is known as a corporate culture. Traditionally, it has been communicated by displaying mission statements. For instance, Starbucks corporation has the following mission statement displayed under its logo:

"To inspire and nurture the human spirit – one person, one cup and one neighborhood at a time."

Human spirit is a Value and the Goals are to inspire and nurture it. These are commonly referred to as advertised values. They are often used to attract investors and employees. Changes in corporate culture can change the way the companies conduct their business. In turn, changes in business practices often effect profits and employee retention. For example, imagine a service department of an IT company that is now directed to upsell products and services during interactions with customers. Service techs, while excellent at what they do, are not interested, and probably not trained or skilled, at sales. Therefore, they may comply in the short run and contribute to a spike in revenues and profits. Nevertheless, should the pressure to sell stay high, some service techs may look for opportunities elsewhere. The costs associated with turnover will cut into profits. Wall Street has provided a great case for us to look at next.

At the time of his resignation, Goldman Sachs's Vice President Greg Smith wrote "…culture was always a vital part of Goldman Sachs's success. It revolved around teamwork, integrity, a spirit of humility, and always doing right by our clients. The culture was the secret sauce that made this place great and allowed us to earn our client's trust for over 143 years…I am sad to say that I look around today and see virtually no trace of the culture that made me love working for this firm for many years…I no longer have pride, or the belief." [1]

The influence of corporate culture on company's goal setting or, in terms of the Four Wheel Alignment Model, the relationship between the Values Wheel and Goals Wheel, has been studied by many economists. In one such study, integrity was defined as business choices that are not based on today's opportunity for profits at the expense of customer satisfaction.[2] Below are some of the important observations that were made.

1. "Contrary to expectation, neither the presence of the founder, nor the nature of customers is correlated with the level of integrity." [This observation was made regarding publically traded companies and demystifies the notion that Integrity is maintained by the presence of the founder after the company goes public.]

2. "When we look at CEO compensation…we find a positive and statistically significant correlation with Integrity. A higher compensation can be both the sign of a very valuable CEO and/or of a very entrenched one. Either way, it is a sign that the CEO has more power vis-à-vis the

shareholders and thus she is better able – if she wants to - to maintain the integrity value even at the expense of a lower short term profit." [It is important to notice the "if she wants to" clause. The power to maintain the Integrity is there! It is a matter of choice.]

3. Summarizing the rest of the study, the culture of Integrity was weaker among publically traded companies compared to privately held companies. Additionally, making decisions based on Integrity showed positive correlation with long term profit.

When employee retention becomes an important Goal for a company, understanding what drives job satisfaction is essential. Many companies get it wrong when they think salary and bonuses are the main contributors to job satisfaction. In fact, salary has no correlation to job satisfaction. The two-factor theory, developed in the 1950's by Frederick Herzberg, separates job satisfaction and job dissatisfaction into two categories. See Figure 2.1.

Fig. 2.1

HERZBERG'S TWO FACTOR THEORY

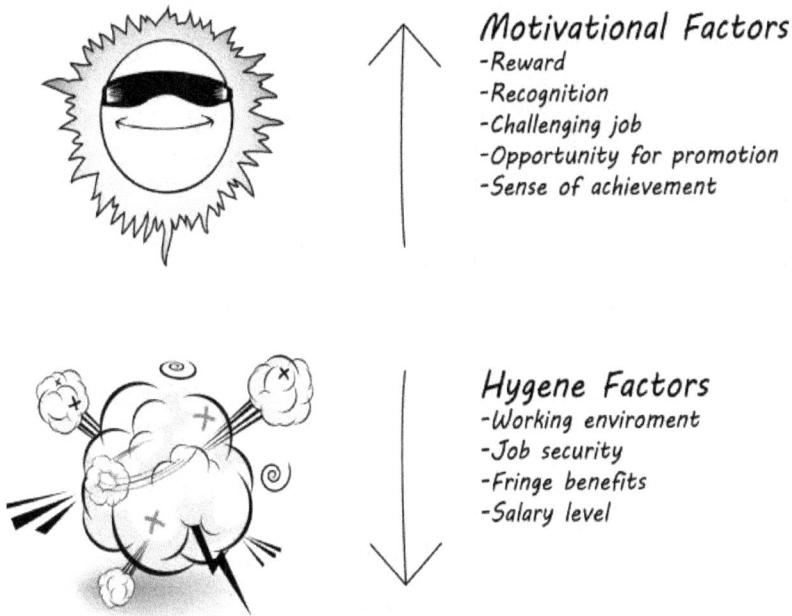

Motivational Factors
-Reward
-Recognition
-Challenging job
-Opportunity for promotion
-Sense of achievement

Hygene Factors
-Working enviroment
-Job security
-Fringe benefits
-Salary level

Job satisfaction has to do with the job itself. Job satisfaction increases with the increase in motivational factors such as opportunities to learn and grow, being recognized, and the impact of the job inside and outside of the organization. Motivational factors do not include salary, bonuses, or benefits. That's why we see army soldiers, policemen, and fire-fighters risking their lives. None of them have chosen their occupations to become rich. Instead, motivation comes from the challenges and pride for being able to work for the greater good.

Job dissatisfaction has to do with the working environment. The factors of job dissatisfaction are called hygiene factors. They include salary, benefits, relationship with bosses and co-workers, culture, morale, size of the office, and quality of office furniture. At its best, these factors minimize job dissatisfaction.

That's why we see some high paying professionals leaving their toxic bosses and soul-sucking jobs to pursue occupational goals of significance.

It may seems odd that job satisfaction and job dissatisfaction are not on the same plane because the words "satisfaction" and "dissatisfaction" sound like antonyms. To illustrate the difference of domains, let's look at the two-factor theory through a framework of another, also known as Maslow's theory of needs hierarchy.

Developed about a decade prior to the two-factor theory by Herzberg, the original hierarchy of needs is depicted in Figure 2.2 below.

Fig 2.2

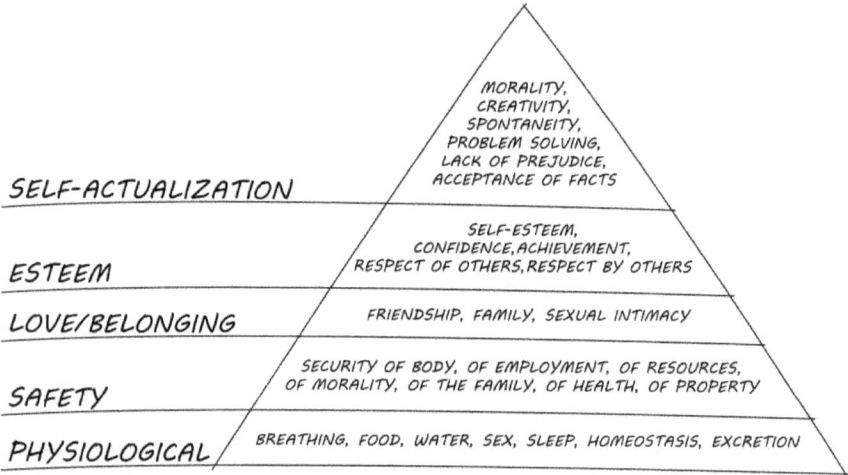

SELF-ACTUALIZATION — MORALITY, CREATIVITY, SPONTANEITY, PROBLEM SOLVING, LACK OF PREJUDICE, ACCEPTANCE OF FACTS

ESTEEM — SELF-ESTEEM, CONFIDENCE, ACHIEVEMENT, RESPECT OF OTHERS, RESPECT BY OTHERS

LOVE/BELONGING — FRIENDSHIP, FAMILY, SEXUAL INTIMACY

SAFETY — SECURITY OF BODY, OF EMPLOYMENT, OF RESOURCES, OF MORALITY, OF THE FAMILY, OF HEALTH, OF PROPERTY

PHYSIOLOGICAL — BREATHING, FOOD, WATER, SEX, SLEEP, HOMEOSTASIS, EXCRETION

The first two levels represent the needs to be met for one to survive. The third level is really the first when it comes to creating an environment where one can grow and prosper. It has been said that humans are social animals and we need others for friendship and love, to create families of our own, and to give to and to receive from. The last two levels are

38

individual needs of a higher order, or Values that can only be achieved when the lower order needs are mostly met.

Combining both theories in Figure 2.3 helps to show why job dissatisfaction is not the beginning of a continuum that ends with job satisfaction. Each term is on its own plane. Moreover, there is a space in-between satisfied and dissatisfied. According to one 2015 survey of 838 Public Relation professionals in public, private, corporate, and nonprofit sectors, 11% of respondents were "neither satisfied nor dissatisfied." [3]

Fig. 2.3

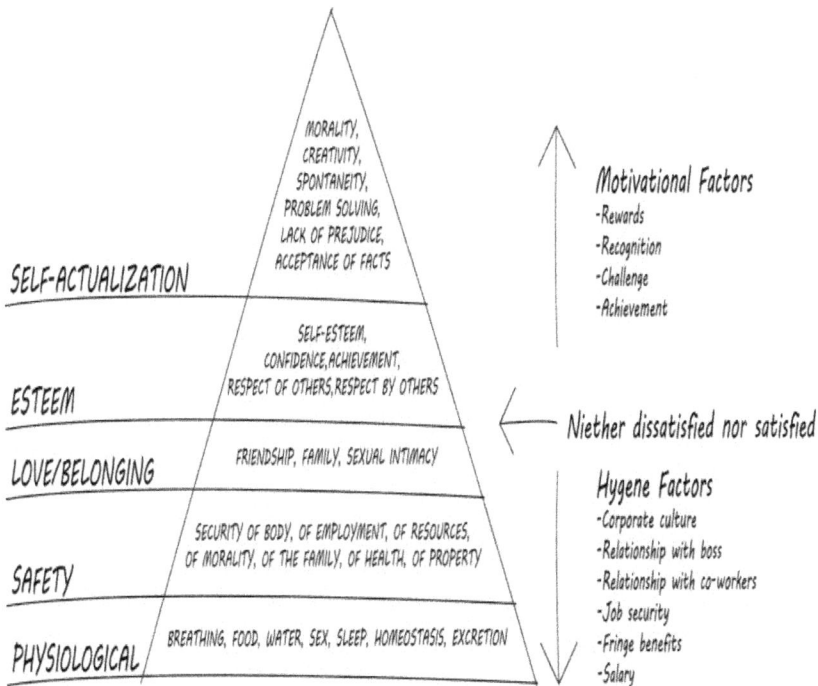

A career choice is often a reflection of an individual's values. Before accepting a position, the potential employee must decide whether a particular job fits the bigger picture of a career they are trying to build. To test this hypothesis, a study was conducted.[4] 192 students from business, economics, and public administration departments completed surveys that tested the relationship between eight career attributes (technical, independence, entrepreneurship, security, administrative, private life, competitiveness, and respectability) and five individual values (silence, universalism, achievement, positivism and individuality). Through the regression analysis that controlled for demographic variables, the value of achievement correlated the strongest with all the career attributes. A sense of achievement is also one of the aspects of job satisfaction. That said, not everyone receives solid career advice that is based on individual's values.

Over the years I have observed a few friends and acquaintances that led their lives by making very logical, yet reactive, decisions. Since I could not survey them at the time they were making these decisions, I can only guess that living an independent life was a goal of high significance. Truth be told, I was one of them. However, there are hidden dangers in careers that at first glance appear very attractive.

The danger of becoming a commodity.

When living an independent life becomes a reality, the price of rent, owning a car, buying groceries, and buying clothing can quickly add up to a monthly sum that requires an annual salary of $50,000 or more. This, in turn, puts pressure on career choices that promise the highest earning potential in the shortest amount of time.

According to the US Bureau of Labor Statistics, these are some of the career choices with the highest earning potential that do not require a college degree.[5]

- Real Estate Agent: Top earning potential of $110,560 or more

- Web Developer / Designer: Top earning potential of $116,620 or more

40

- Commercial Pilot: Top earning potential of $147,890 or more

Attractive earning potential may create a supply of applicants that exceeds the demand in certain markets. A web developer may be able to telecommute, but the competition for these jobs may be even higher.

From a consumer point-of-view, the more service providers that are available, the more the service becomes a commodity. Who wants to feel easily replaceable? When stress and anxiety enter our jobs, they lose their original appeal. Stress may come from the uncertainty that comes from the fear of positions being eliminated, or the nature of work itself, or both. Thus, I have decided to take a further look into the above occupations to see just how stressful they are.

A surprising discovery.

According to the 2016 Jobs Rated report, the stress index of an airline pilot exceeds that of a police officer and is almost identical to that of a fire-fighter.

An interesting study conducted by National Occupational Mortality Surveillance collects data that ranks occupations and the number of suicides. According to 2014 data, Real Estate Agents made the "top 10" with the likelihood of suicide of 1.38 times the average citizen. Their stress level was ranked as 6 out of 10.

Web Developer jobs, according to CareerCast, are the most stressful in the IT industry. The stress comes from the job itself as well as from handling demanding clients.

This may sound as though I have purposely chosen these three examples to show a correlation between high potential salaries and high levels of stress. I have not. Some of the data I saw as I was looking up the reports made my jaw drop more than once. I've come to realize that any career will have its "true cost" that we would have to pay. Unless we know someone in the occupation or do our own research, we may not be aware of some downsides. Choosing occupations based solely on earning potential may not be a good idea. Looking back at the two-factor theory, salary and fringe benefits are associated with the level of job dissatisfaction, while challenge and recognition are associated with job satisfaction. This explains why soldiers, policemen, and firefighters, as an example, are willing to risk their lives. For these individuals, motivational factors are far more significant than hygiene factors.

Profit / Loss Exercise

To test the Significance of Goals, I like this simple "Profit / Loss" exercise. When considering a certain goal, consider answering two questions in list form. The first list would answer the question "What is my Profit if I attain this goal?" The second list would answer the question "What is my Loss if I don't attain this goal?" Ideally, we want as many answers to each question as possible. We can take breaks and come back to questions to really push a critical type of thinking towards our Goals.

Meaning.

When it comes to personal Goals, it would be a gross oversight not to talk about a subject matter that preoccupied great philosophers, scientists, and writers for many centuries. In terms of The Four Wheel Alignment Model, this subject matter has to do with a relationship between one's Goals and one's Beliefs about one's identity. *Who am I?* To answer this question with information other than indicated on a business card or a resume, one would have to look deep inside. The answer to this question is the first step towards a certain goal that in itself is a journey of discovery of life's best kept secrets. Some believe that it is the same for all, others believe that it is unique to each individual. Sooner or later we ask ourselves a question, directly or indirectly, about this one very important aspect of our life. We ask ourselves about life's meaning.

There is no shortage of schools of thoughts or philosophical perspectives that tackle, or attempt to tackle, the meaning of life. In Western society alone, there were about 20 major philosophical movements starting with Platonism of Ancient Greece through modern day Postmodernism. Additionally, meaning of life perspectives are offered by all religions and by popular culture. The complexity of and contradictions between the perspectives would make a novice seeker of meaning wondering how subscribing to a certain idea and sticking with it is possible.

From a bird's-eye view on the diversity of answers, I'd like to offer what I see as relevant to the topics we have covered thus far. Below are three points to consider. First, I will briefly outline them. Second, I'll explain what's relevant to the coaching process. Finally, we'll dive into each topic.

1. Lifelong learners. Often, the meaning of life is something that is unlikely to be attained in one's lifetime (i.e. great wisdom) or has to do with something that is larger than the self (i.e. God).

2. Causality of changes. The meaning of life often changes as a result of changes in individuals and environments. We can look at changes in individuals and environments as a chicken-or-the-egg causality argument, or as a two-way street possibility.

3. Alignment between the front Wheels. It does not matter how we come to embrace a certain answer, idea, or a perspective on the meaning of life, what matters is how well we align our Beliefs to the corresponding Goals.

Two thoughts before the dive:

1.   As a coach, I am more interested in the "here and now" of a client's Beliefs and Goals. They do not have to fall into any particular movement, religion, or culture in order for the coaching process to work. Once Goals and the corresponding Values are identified, the movement toward achieving the agreed-upon Goals becomes the priority.

2.   All the possible explanations of life's meaning call for some sort of action. The thought of an action, before materializing into action, is a task. Like a line that connects the dots, actions connect tasks on our "to do" lists. As we spend time thinking about the possible outcomes of actions taken over a period of time, eventually, we start seeing a path to achieving Goals. Thinking is just as critical as doing.

1. Lifelong Learners.

When we attend school, we are graded based on the answers we provide on quizzes, tests, and examinations. The answers fall into four categories: right, wrong, good, or bad. The right or wrong answers had to do with calculations, while good or bad answers were to the types of questions that required a display of critical thinking (such as an essay written on a controversial topic). Graduating with high school diplomas and college degrees gave us a sense of being ready to take on the world. All that we were supposed to learn about the world and achieve the minimum required level of mastery has been learned and achieved, as evidenced by diplomas we were holding in our hands. The commencement speech acknowledges that as well. We, therefore, were promised a place and career in life. Life just became meaningful. This is precisely the line of thinking that get us in trouble as we enter our first full-time job and start our careers.

Witnessing the struggles of parents, as they worked hard to make ends meet, or encountering life challenges of our own, we eventually realize that what we learned in classrooms can't help. That made us question the promise we received of a good and fair life. Often arriving in our mid-to-late-twenties, we conclude what we once knew and held as high Beliefs are no longer serving us. It's time to try something else.

In search of something more substantial than what pop culture and traditional education have to offer, some turn their sights to religion. It offers time-tested Values and provides guidance to life's meaning. All of a sudden, the void produced by the lack of answers is starting to get filled and we feel, among other things, wiser. We are now able to solve a problem for which there was no right, wrong, good, or bad answer. Recovering from bruises, we hope we got it right this time and there will be no need to deal with painful change again.

We will talk about what the passing grade of a life lesson looks like in the next chapter. Usually, it takes a few failing grades to make us wiser. After a few decades of trial and error, most of us will come to appreciate the bittersweet taste of wine and life, and that's how we become lifelong learners.

2. Causality of Changes.

War, revolution, immigration, natural disaster, change in marital status, motor vehicle accidents, birth or death of a family member: these are all examples of dramatic changes in an environment over a short period of time. Individuals involved have to react to a new reality by reconsidering their Values. For example, if a family lost their home to a natural disaster or war, securing a safe dwelling will be a higher priority than keeping professional or social commitments.

At the same time, many changes to our environment are caused by the actions of a small or a large group of individuals that pursue similar Goals. Typically, these changes take a longer period of time to materialize. Plans of war and revolts are, typically, kept secret. Scientific breakthroughs may be decades in the making before a new technology becomes an "overnight success." Even at the individual level, it may take years before one proposes marriage or decides to file for a divorce.

When we think about changes in individuals and environments with which the individuals interact as a point in time, it may look like a two-way street. We are in constant interaction with our environment and vice versa. When we think about changes in individuals and environments as a chain of events over a longer period of time, similar to the way a historian looks at major events, we might start to think that because one event took place before another, that the earlier event caused the later.

A great deal of time is spent arguing about changes in history, science, family matters, and so forth. For some, the arguing itself becomes a way of life, and winning as many arguments as possible becomes life's meaning. Still, for most, changes to a large enough number of Beliefs will lead to changes in a large enough number of Goals. The changes in the Beliefs and Goals Wheels will result in changes in the overall direction in life. To illustrate this metaphor, look at Figure 1.1 and imagine the front wheels turning.

3. Alignment Between the Front Wheels.

Change in our lives has different impacts. Most changes are minor, like a new version of software or a faster-running operating system of a smartphone. Although, over a period of time, these small changes in communication technology may alter the way we interact with others in a social or professional setting. Even then, these changes do not result in changes in our core Beliefs and Values. There are other changes in our lives that are more impactful and will test our core Beliefs and Values. Those two types of changes are:

- Prolonged continuing small changes that eventually result in a change of the overall direction or moral compass. Take someone who started as an honest young professional and tries to rationalize the cause of becoming a corrupt professional over time. What core Beliefs must have changed to set the corresponding Goals of seeking opportunities to take advantage of certain situations?

- A dramatic event that almost instantly alters our core Beliefs and Values. In this case, the overall experience is more dramatic due to lack of time available to adjust to a new reality. The changes to core Beliefs are often necessary to address survival and safety. Physiologically and psychologically, the individuals may be traumatized and it may take months or even years to recover.

Acknowledging the many possibilities and types of changes as well as their origins has nothing to do with the necessity of making adjustments to Goals accordingly. Known as cognitive dissonance, a situation where conflicting Beliefs coexist and result in internal distress, is a great example of what may happen when older Beliefs and the new ones are not given careful consideration. Without first sorting out the Beliefs, our Goals may also become conflicting. In the Model, the Wheel of Beliefs and Values and the Wheel of Goals form a front axis. The Wheels are responsible for the direction we travel. Therefore, both should be pointing in the same directions, especially at higher speeds.

In conclusion, we get to decide the meaning of our lives. We can certainly adopt one of many philosophical or religious views. The views may and often change over the course of our lives. To live our lives in harmony, we must set Goals that reflect the meaning as we see it. One of the larger Goals that follows obtaining clarity of meaning is purpose.

Purpose.

The reality is we don't take the time to think about life's meaning and purpose. We may occasionally ask the question, but will not commit time and willpower to finding the answer. We'd rather wait for something else to come along that would take our focus away from the challenge of discovering the purpose. Therefore, we are going to work on discovering the purpose right now! This will be a superset consisting of two exercises.

Exercise 1

Below are some questions that will help you to think about your purpose. Don't think about the question, concentrate on your answer. Write the question and the answer on a sheet of paper so that you can come back to it later. Most importantly, take your time answering these questions.

1. If you did not have a job, how would you choose to fill time?

2. What activity makes you lose track of time?

3. What kind of world challenges do you find yourself being attracted to the most?

4. What are you passionate about today?

5. Who are you?

6. Want do you want?

7. Why do you want it?

At the moment, we are not concerned with anything other than discovering the Purpose. Review your answers and get ready for the second exercise.

Exercise 2

In the gym of life coaching, there are hundreds of exercises available. I have selected one that truly represents an essence of life coaching. Experiencing negative thoughts such as doubts and fear is normal. It is when they get in the way of achieving our goals that we find ourselves stuck. This exercise may help. It is called "Changing your Beliefs." [6]

1. On the top of a fresh sheet of paper in your journal, write down your negative thought or belief.

2. Under the belief, write down all the ways that this belief has cost you in your life. Write how this belief has affected you in the past, how it is currently affecting you, and how it will affect you in the future if you continue to hold on to this belief. Try to write without stopping. Do not spend time thinking about it and make sure to write from your heart. Write whatever comes to you, even if it seems crazy. While you write, experience all the emotions that come up. This is crucial. Keep writing until you cannot think of anything else to write about the topic. Then, repeat this exercise by writing all of the benefits you get from this belief.

3. After you have made your list, assign a number to each item. These numbers will refer to the amount of pain that you associate with the particular item in the list. The number is completely arbitrary, so just use the first

49

number that comes to your mind. When you have assigned a number to each item, add all the numbers together and write their sum at the bottom of the paper.

4. Repeat step 3 by assigning a number to each item on your benefit list. The costs and benefits lists will each have a separate point total.

5. Now take your negative belief and rewrite it so that it becomes empowering. For example, if the original belief was "I do not have what it takes to be successful because I always screw things up," your new belief may be "Mistakes are a part of life, and by learning to improve I will succeed."

6. Write this new belief on a fresh sheet of paper and repeat the exercise. Only this time, you will write down all the ways that you believe you will benefit from your new belief as well as any cost for adopting it. Assign a point value to each item.

7. When you are done, review your lists and compare the point totals. For your negative belief, how does the point total for the costs compare with that of the benefits? For your new belief, how does the point total for the benefits compare with the point total of the costs?

8. Review your list each day for a week, remembering to feel your emotions as you read them. Doing this will reinforce in your mind all the costs that you are incurring under your current belief and all the benefits of adopting your new one.

Going through this superset should help to bring to the forefront a more clear purpose and more positive Beliefs. This will also help to align the Wheel of Goals to the Wheel of Beliefs and Values.

Passion or Purpose?

Titles like Passion & Purpose and Passion vs. Purpose have been featured in too many books and blogs to not catch our attention. Sometimes, the two are used interchangeably. Ouch! I think a bit of clarification and direction is in order.

Passion is a strong emotion of enthusiasm or excitement. Emotions are short-lived feelings. Both emotions and feelings often change their sources. For example, we can be just as happy or sad when watching a movie or eating an ice cream. We can feel joy or sadness in the moment and for no obvious reason. Happiness or sadness may be caused by a thought that came to our mind at the same time as we were watching a movie or eating an ice cream. This is how emotions work. They come and go, they can be fleeting. They may have a reason, and they may not. Therefore, Passion, being an emotion-based concept, is neither sustainable, nor specific to Beliefs and Goals that are aligned with a purpose.

When we make statements of passion like "I am really passionate about my work," we may be lying to ourselves. Or, at least, we are technically being inaccurate since our work, in reality, is a source of a large range of emotions and feelings, from frustration and stress to joy and happiness. We cannot be enthused about only certain parts of work that happen once in a while. A better statement of positive affirmation regarding work, that we find truly in alignment with our Beliefs of our life's purpose, is "I find a great deal of purpose in what I do, regardless of challenges!"

During my teenage years, I attended a college of music where I met and became a close friend with a talented young individual. His name is Vladimir Mogilevsky. As often happens after college, life got complicated for both of us and we lost contact for 15 years. When we finally reconnected, Vladimir had become an award-winning pianist with an impressive repertoire of 26 programs, 90-120 minutes each. He traveled the world and settled in Dusseldorf, Germany. Over the past ten years, we have reconnected and talk frequently over the phone and Skype. Technology made it easier to stay in touch. As I am typing these words, I got Vladimir's permission to talk about his life via a message that came over WhatsApp.

Vladimir has a very passionate presence on stage. He is best known as a performer of Romantic-era composers such as Chopin, Liszt, Schubert, and Rachmaninoff. His body language and facial expressions are in total accord with the music his powerful hands and an impeccable technique create. All of his concerts, public and private, go well beyond the scope of the official program as his audience wants to experience more of the passion that he generates. Playing three to five encore pieces is his norm with an even longer performance being a frequent exception.

While the feedback that Vladimir would receive from music critics and the audience would be positive, he has shared with me that some people from the general audience believed that once he became a masterful pianist, he could enjoy the rest of his live traveling, playing, and being admired. That he would be able to just relax and live a life of passion! This erroneous conclusion is easy to make when all you see is him performing on a stage of Festspielhouse in Baden-Baden, Germany's largest opera and concert venue and receiving a standing ovation from 2,500 adoring fans.

Knowing Vladimir as long as I have, I can tell you that his passionate presence has nothing to do with his life's purpose. He has chosen a life of service to music. He considers himself as a medium between the composers and the audience. I am a witness who can give you a first-hand account of the tremendous amount of time he invested in his craft as a pianist. His commitment to mastery goes above and beyond what I would consider normal or, maybe even healthy. Strong in his service commitment, yet vulnerable to life outside of music, Vladimir endured many hardships but stayed true to the purpose he chose for himself. I think his story best illustrates the difference between passion and purpose.

Service as Purpose.

A practical way to discover our purpose is to adopt and hold in high regards a Value of service. Think of pharaohs, kings, queens, and presidents. These are all examples of servant leaders. Obviously, not all the world leaders went down in history as great public servants; however, that's how high-level leaders have been perceived for centuries. They were looked up to by the nations to make the world a better place. If the situation required so, common people were ready to sacrifice their lives to further a cause identified by their leaders.

Notwithstanding power that comes to one by the virtue of dynasty, appointment, election, or a revolt, the life of service is equally available to people of any occupation and socio-economic status. Here is how I see the process of aligning Beliefs and Goals that brings Service into the focus. When answering the questions below, take time to think through and identify an area of service in either the real or fictitious life of your hero:

1. Who is my hero?

2. What does my hero believe in?

3. What kind of goals does my hero have?

Replace your hero's name with your own and repeat questions two and three keeping in mind the idea of service. Do you see a commonality in Beliefs and Goals that you and your hero have? If so, wouldn't it make sense to become a hero yourself and dedicate your life to the ideals that you and your hero have in common?

While some heroes, at least superheroes, live in a fantasy world and have superpowers, what they fight for must ring true for those who spent time and money reading books, collecting comics, action figures, and watching the movies. Ask yourself "What's the attraction?" Personally, I wonder if the answer lies in a superheroes' abilities to do what we can't.

A life of service does not require superpowers or high office. It does require, however, a Belief and a Goal that is larger than and outside of one's self. One could choose to service a local community by donating time, mentoring, building, or planting trees. What would make such activity different from what we would perceive as a promotion is an intent and expectation. When we truly serve, we would plant the trees, for example, because we believe that trees contribute to fresher air and we expect nothing in return. Obviously, there will have to be a balancing act between what we do for a living today, and what we just found out may be our purpose (i.e. planting trees).

Another option to live a life of Service is to choose a career of service. Such careers include public safety, education, firefighters, police, and emergency and disaster responders. The list is quite long and also includes the fields of education, science, medicine, foreign service, and religion. (See Figure 2.4) Do you ever wonder how people end up choosing these various career paths? Perhaps, you know someone and already know the answer. Perhaps this person is you. In this case, I'd like to take this opportunity and say "thank you for your service!"

For me, coaching offered an opportunity to serve others in a way that is similar to a career in education. My coaching journey that started with formal coaching training has not stopped after graduation. The value of learning and applying new skills resonates with many of my clients who are lifelong learners. My service comes in the form of broadcasting the following message: "you, at this time, have all you need to become the best version of yourself, to live your life to the fullest, to bring forward your personal and professional mastery, and to experience more positivity in all that you do." In a short amount of time, I have spent hundreds of hours in creating content and materials and sharing it with groups and individuals with a sole purpose of explaining what true coaching is and what it is not. I will continue doing so with absolutely no expectations of being compensated, praised, or acknowledged for the efforts in any way. This is not a part of my "coaching business," this is a part of my personality. I believe that someone in some way will benefit from a word I utter, in a passage I write, or in my videos someone may stumble upon on the Internet. This Belief has shaped a few new Goals that took time and financial resources away from other Goals. As the result, for the past 12 months my life took on a whole new meaning and Purpose and I have been experiencing life with more harmony with myself and with others.

Chapter Summary.

The Beliefs and Values and Goals Wheels are front Wheels, (see Figure 1.1) and steer us throughout our life journey. Therefore, the importance of a strong alignment between them is hard to overestimate. Anyone who is involved in tire sales and services will tell you that the front tires of your car or truck will wear faster than your rear tires because of a combined effect of steering and weight distribution during braking. These same forces work similarly in my metaphoric presentation of Beliefs and Values as they relate to Goals.

Corporate culture, as we have examined, is centered on the values that come from management and owners. Often, the advertised values used to attract talent have very little to do with what is really going on inside the organization. We looked at a case study of Goldman Sachs and concluded that corporate culture in general, and that of Integrity, is not directly caused by either the presence of a founder, or the compensation of a CEO. In both cases, it is a matter of a choice between a) maintenance of the value of Integrity by making a Goal of doing so a priority or b) making quarterly profits a priority that is higher than Integrity.

As hard as it may seem to maintain a healthy corporate culture, it only goes so far when it comes to employee retention, as corporate culture is only one of several hygiene factors, as described in two-factor theory. Even the best corporate culture does not provide much motivation. Employees will always seek motivators in a particular job or a career path. Ultimately, the employees are seeking significance in what they do. Significance is the relationship and the alignment factor between the Wheel of Beliefs and Values and the Wheel of Goals.

Another important relationship between the Wheels of Beliefs and Goals is meaning. Hardly any other search in the history of mankind could rival in its relentlessness as a search for life's meaning. Dozens of philosophical and religious schools of thought on the subject matter are available for an individual to adopt. Alternatively, we can proactively define our meaning of life. As a side note, we acknowledged our interactions with environments, similar to the tires constantly hitting the road bumps, big and small, that eventually may lead to the Beliefs and Values Wheel getting out of alignment with the Goals Wheel, thereby loosing Meaning.

Synonymous with meaning, purpose is another way to align the Beliefs and Goals Wheels. An exercise, if given the proper time and effort, in finding our purpose, should prove helpful. Purpose, not to be confused with passion, which has its roots in strong emotions, not thoughts, takes on several forms. One of them, service, is examined further.

Finally, service is a practical option within the same category of alignment as meaning and purpose. Regardless of socio-economic status, we can pursue a life of service in various fields and with different levels of time commitment: from an occasional volunteerism to a lifelong career in service.

Fig. 2.4

PUBLIC SERVICE CAREERS

Chapter Three: Relationship Between the Wheels of Beliefs and Values and Actions.

For ease of reference, throughout this chapter, I will be referring to the Beliefs and Values Wheel as the Beliefs Wheel or Beliefs.

Before we act, we need to believe we can do it. At the same time, by doing things we can change what we believe we can do. Therefore, the first part of this chapter will focus on the correlation between Beliefs and Actions.

Remember when you were little and your parents would ask you "Why did you do that?" Perhaps, when you were little, you had posed the same question to your parents, grandparents, friends, and even strangers. Either way, the response to this question is aimed to discover a reason for our Actions. Reason is a one-way direction from the Beliefs Wheel to the Actions Wheel and this is our next stop.

Reason.

For a comprehensive view, we will have to jump off the cliff and dive into some deep waters. We won't be covering the entire ocean of philosophical and psychological works and theories. Nevertheless, understanding the "Big Three" of reason is worth our time and analysis.

1. Normative

2. Motivational

3. Explanatory

During a coaching session, when a client talks about a situation which is posing a challenge, the word choice he or she uses represents not only the objects with their properties but the logical connections between them—such as correlation or causality. Understanding the way a client sees the situation and either working within that existing framework of Beliefs, or having the client realize that the existing framework is no longer of value and a new framework is essential for a successful change in Actions. For, as Henry Ford put it, "if you always do what you've always done, you'll always get what you've always got." By examining different mental reasoning, you may come to a realization, a new way of thinking about your own situation. Should this happen, you may even try a different course of Action!

1. Normative Reasons.

Each society has its own set of norms that range in a somewhat objective hierarchy of importance. For example, the Constitution is generally thought of as being more important than a Code of Ethics that a new employee receives from their HR Department. Legal norms, in terms of the hierarchy, are residing somewhere between the Constitution and the Code of Ethics. In addition to the concept of normative reasons, there are normative ethics, normative claims, normative social influence, and normative economics.

Regardless of a particular concept, normative is when words like "shall," "should," or "ought;" as well as "shall not," "should not," and the less common "ought not" are used, in conjunction with verbs, to form a list of standards or values. "Thou shalt not kill" is an example of a norm. Equally true in its normative properties is the expression "When feeling ill, one should see a doctor." What makes it true is a common acceptance of doctors as a source of curing illnesses.

In addition to "should" and "should not," norms are also expressed by comparative expressions like "better than" and "worse than." These comparative expressions indicate a relationship between the norm and the location of an event on the scale of normality. For example, good driving weather is defined as "sunny, no wind, with a temperature range of 50F - 80F." Rain would be considered a less than good driving condition. However, based on the actual statistics of car accidents that are caused by various driving conditions, rain can also be expressed as worse than a good driving condition, but better than ice because braking and steering on ice is far less effective. This rational makes the rainy condition better than an icy condition and may even justify keeping our travel plans. Also known as the lesser of two evils principle, it is used to justify Actions.

Justification. There are a number of heated debates around moral and ethical applications of the principle of justification. We will not go further into them in this book, but make a mental note that the principle of the lesser of two evils is a part of normative reasoning.

It also should be noted that normative reasoning has a factual and informative element to it. For example, it is perfectly normal for a host to serve food to guests. It is also assumed by the guests that the host would not serve bad or tainted food. When we act, it is assumed by other people that we know what we are doing and why. Therefore, we consider all the information or facts prior to acting. We make sure our Actions, based on our factual knowledge, will be within the norms and can be explained by normative reasoning.

Finally, it is important to acknowledge other sources for norms such as popular culture, country-specific traditions and customs, various religious movements and cults, and even codes of conduct within organized crime organizations. All these norms exist, on one hand, to regulate our Actions and make them in Alignment with normative Beliefs. On the other hand, the norms are useful guides that are up to our choosing. How we choose our actual course of action is still a subject of much discussion. The reasons that we use to explain why we do what we do are called motivational reasons.

2. Motivational Reasons.

Some of our Beliefs motivate us more than others. Referring to these motivators, we say "that's what makes me tick!" These internal motivators drive our everyday Actions. These Actions are performed on a regular basis and on those occasions when we think no one is looking. Running a red light is an example of the second type of Action. We may be well aware of the traffic laws, or norms. Still, motivated by Beliefs that being late to a meeting might cost us way more than a ticket and, potentially, an increase in an auto insurance premium, we might consider the odds of being caught by police low enough to be in favor of running a red light.

In the example above, we again see the use of information. First, we know that we are running late. Second, we don't see any police around. Additionally, we believe that a) should we stop at the red light we will be late for a meeting, b) being late for a meeting will cost us a job promotion, and c) since we do not see any police around, we will not get caught. Lastly, we make a Value call between the potential negative outcomes. In this example, we favored motivational reason over normative. At the same time, what motivates us does not have to be in conflict with the norms.

Simply put, the difference between the normative and motivational reasons is the source of "permission" for an action. If it came from an outside source, i.e. a green traffic light, it is a normative reason. If something inside of us gave us a reason to act, that something was motivation. Outside motivators, such as social media advertisements or motivational speakers, must connect with our inside set of motivating Beliefs to cause Action.

Have you noticed how in most thrillers, a search for a perpetrator starts with a list of all the suspects and ends with the most likely individual based on the criteria of motive?

Motivational reason to commit a crime is held in such a high regard that it rivals with other processes such as finding factual evidence to support guilty claims. If someone could have a motive to commit a crime, but lacking factual evidence, planting a weapon or other evidence can easily steer an investigation into the wrong direction.

Sometimes, we may get motivated by reasons that have no factual support. For instance, if motivated only by our Belief that a certain course of action will provide for the desired outcome, we may embark on a new business endeavor. Not having enough information, experience, or financial backing causes so many start-ups to fail. Not having a back-up plan causes individuals to undergo financial hardships, including filing for bankruptcy. When it comes to tangible matters, believing in something is no substitute for factual evidence. Even the best of business plans followed by an impeccable execution will not guarantee success. Factual support is the basis for explanatory reasons.

3. Explanatory Reasons.

Explanatory reasons answer "why" questions but in a way that neither assumes moral or ethical judgment, nor relies on Beliefs. Explanatory reasons simply state the facts and offer either a correlation or causality between them. You may even think of these reasons as scientific.

Let's consider the example of four wheel alignment for your car. The owner's manual may suggest that under normal operating conditions, you should get your wheels aligned every 24 months or 24,000 miles. This suggestion gives you a normative reason to do the alignment. You may get a coupon in the mail that offers a great discount on four wheel alignment and you might be close to the 24,000-mile mark, or even over it. However, it is the discount that will give you a motivational reason to turn your car in for service. It is important to note that in either case, the actual condition of the tires, the very reason to have your wheel alignment checked and maintained in the first place, has not been taken into consideration. Depending on facts such as the brand of your tires, your driving style, road conditions, and the condition of your car's suspension, the amount, and type of tire wear will vary. When you make your decision to turn your car in based on the tire wear, if, for instance, the front tires are showing more wear on the outside, you are using explanatory reasons.

Understanding these different types of reasons is necessary if we are trying to explain our Actions as well as the Actions of others. The effort too is well worth it as it will provide you with more insights and "aha" moments. While this understanding is desirable for all, it is a requirement for someone in a leadership role. Great leaders challenge existing norms while providing motivating reasons for us to act in a way that is aligned with certain Goals and Values. Cultural changes in companies are good examples of a behavioral change that requires leadership and understanding of normative and motivational reasons.

Before we look at a case study, I'd like to illustrate how companies, by making small changes to their culture, or norms, can eventually become the opposite of what they used to be.

Founded in 1913 by Arthur Andersen, Arthur Andersen, LLP was one of the Big Five of accounting firms. Known for its culture of quality and integrity, shortly after A. Anderson passed away in 1947, the company's leaders shifted their priorities from quality and integrity to growing profits and market share. This was a shift in normative reasons to support a new course of Actions.

While expanding its consulting services around the world, Andersen stopped requiring its accountant to spend two years in auditing. At the same time, each new change in norms, however small and rational, made it possible to do things that would not have been possible 20 or 30 years prior. As a result, when Four Seasons Nursing Centers of America filed for bankruptcy in 1973, the founder pleaded guilty to securities fraud and two partners and one employee of Arthur Andersen & Co. were indicted.[1]

After this incident, the company continued on its course of lowering accounting standards to justify questionable practices that ultimately resulted in being part of the Enron scandal in the late 1990s. Despite the fact that two of the last three Comptrollers General of the Government Accountability Office were top executives of Arthur Andersen, the company's demise was unavoidable. Once a giant of 113,000 employees worldwide, in 2007 Arthur Andersen had only a single location and a few hundred employees with its primary focus being on training professionals for other larger companies. According to the company's website, arthurandersenco.com, as of June 1, 2016 Arthur Andersen is pursuing a goal of enlisting 100 affiliates by the year 2020. (At the time of this book's publication in 2017, the official list of affiliates has yet to be published.) Additionally, the website has a Corporate Social Responsibility (or Values) page that displays a picture of the founder and the historic values—some of which are registered trademarks—such as Think Straight, Talk Straight®; Duty, Integrity, Ethics, Trust®; and One Firm, One Voice®. By following the company, we will be able to see what Actions will come out from the stated Values. The future of Arthur Andersen is unfolding before us.

Another example is Aetna, a managed health care company. The culture of this 160-year-old company that started as a life insurance policy provider that has been described by its own employees as conservative, resistant to change, and not really open to cultural diversity. The norms instilled by the executives read "we take care of our people for life, as long as they show up every day and don't cause trouble." [2]

In 1996, Aetna acquired U.S. Healthcare Inc., also a health care provider but with a different corporate culture. In 1990, U.S. Healthcare opened a new customer service facility near Philadelphia. In an effort to promote an efficient corporate culture, a few interesting measures, or norms, were implemented. For instance, memos and meetings were no longer permitted during the business day and uses of titles within the organization were eliminated. The combination of lean operations, innovative culture, and growing revenues made the company financially attractive enough to be purchased by Aetna.

With the merger of the two companies, there also came a merger of two cultures. Some noteworthy takeaways from that experience are:

- Start with existing strengths. Aetna had a strong legacy of great customer service that by the time of the merger was long forgotten. Once reminded, the employees became re-energized and open for further dialog. Focusing on the cultural strength or Values that can get aligned with new Goals, a set of new Actions have to come next.

- Start with small changes in behaviors (Actions). For instance, in a situation where two or three people have to agree or approve a proposal, instead of having a meeting, utilizing email will save time and the exchange of emails serve as minutes and proof of approval. In the case of Aetna, the change was to the 360-degree surveys. Prone to unpleasant surprises, the practice was complemented with an ongoing informal feedback from the people providing input to the survey to those being surveyed. It allowed for behavioral correction prior to the survey and resulted in far fewer surprises.

- Understanding that a change in Beliefs and Values takes a long time is the key. Realistically speaking, it takes years of continuing effort before seeing some significant changes in the mind-set of employees and consistency in new behaviors. By combining formal motivation, i.e. a compensation plan or review process that pays incentives for certain performance, and informal motivation, such as public recognition, new behaviors will solidify new cultural norms. Employees will more likely have normative as well as motivational reasons to act a certain way.

It should come as no surprise that the same three principles outlined above apply when we are looking to make changes in our personal lives. Understanding what our strengths are and what Beliefs are behind them is fundamental in the moments we find ourselves at a crossroads. Knowing ourselves, trusting what we know and what we can do well, in a confident, calm way, will likely result in more positive choices. Beware that in an effort to boost our confidence, we may psych ourselves up into an undesirable zone of arrogance.* Nevertheless, finding core Beliefs is the first step to be followed by Actions to propel our life in a new direction.

Empowered by healthy confidence, we get motivated to start taking small steps in a new direction. The rate of personal changes, unlike changes in a large organization, can be faster. Yet, just like the resistance of the air a speeding car has to overcome, we have a status quo of the loved ones and friends that we may have to address. The status quo comes from the comfort level our close circle of family and friends have with our current position in life, career, or business. Any changes

---

* *That's when we start thinking that we are better than other people and, as the result, start interacting with others as if they are unwelcomed distractions.*

may be seen as a danger to the relationship. Another important aspect of personal change is patience.

It has been said that patience is a virtue. Patience means waiting without knowing for how long. It is hard to come to terms with considering the proliferation of the instant gratification mindset.

Losing our patience, within the framework of personal change, is a step backwards. It leads to old behaviors and self-doubt. In turn, self-doubt invites self-judgment to take hold. As negative as losing patience may seem, acknowledging and honoring the emotional state of being impatient is just as important as long as impatience does not lead to destructive actions.

To improve patience, it is helpful to think about it not as an emotion, which is hard to control, but as a skill. Improving a skill of patience involves controlling the response to the moments of impatience. Start with a 0-10 scale self-assessment. Rate yourself on the following abilities:

- Controlling temper while waiting in long lines at a doctor's office or an airline counter

- Listening to others without interruption, and

- Moving forward even when things get hard.

The way to improve the skill of patience is practice. By practicing our temper management, active listening, and resilience, we get better at being patient.

Patience with ourselves and others leads to more time and energy available for important changes in Actions. New Actions, or changed behaviors, is the key to fortifying our core Beliefs when they are called into question by life's challenges.

***

For the most part, we have defined and examined normative and motivational reasons. Explanatory reasons often sound like motivational reasons. Yet, there is a distinction. Just listen carefully when someone is trying to explain their Actions, especially if the Actions are perceived in a negative way. For an easy example, let's say someone is late for a meeting because of heavy traffic. Obviously, the person never planned to arrive late. There is no normative or motivational reasons for it. The person may be lying and there is a hidden motive. However, let's assume the person is telling the truth, that because of the auto accident that caused a lane closure and traffic delay, it took 20 minutes longer to get to work. In this case we have an explanatory reason.

A less clear distinction between motivational and explanatory reasons are seen when an Action is taken as a response to a certain situation. Let's take cheating for instance. The question someone may ask themselves is "what would I do if my partner cheated on me?" Let's also assume the answer to this question is no different than to the question "what would I do if I found out that my partner cheated on me?" The subtlety between motivational and explanatory reasons in this example is the knowledge of the fact of cheating. Knowledge explains, while jealousy motivates.

Three types of reasons that we have covered in this chapter are normative, motivational, and explanatory. Understanding why we and others act a certain way opens doors to a variety of opportunities and prepares us for challenges ahead. A simple act of distinguishing between cultural norms and internal motivations, which often result in conflicts that give birth to dramatic plots and heroic tales, will explain a good amount of works of classical and contemporary literature, music, and art.

This concludes the exploration of the relationship going in the direction from Wheel of Beliefs to Wheel of Actions. On the other hand, there exists an opposite direction of relationship from the Wheel of Actions to the Wheel of Beliefs. The way they align is through a process called cognition. (See Figure 3.1)

Fig. 3.1

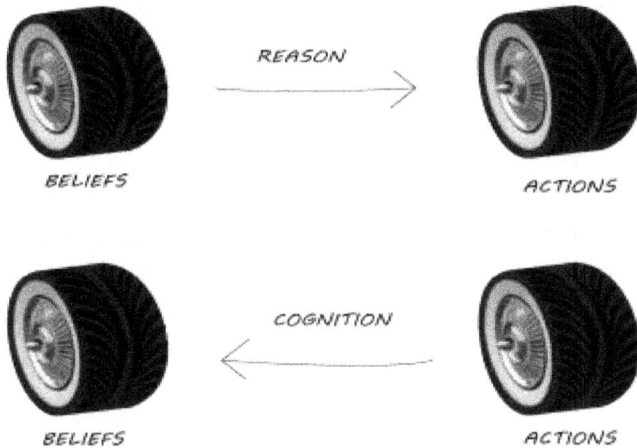

Defined by the Oxford Dictionary as "the mental action or process of acquiring knowledge and understanding through thought, experience, and the senses," cognition itself is a combination of several invisible Actions such as thoughts, feelings, and emotions. (Figure 1.5) Some visible Actions trigger cognitive process more than others. One of these Actions is play.

We are fairly familiar with the importance of play in a child's early development. Learning through play has been employed by psychologists and educators for a long time. The state of Wisconsin was the first in the US to recognize the importance of play in early child development and in 1873 started the first four-year-old kindergarten program. Fast forward to September of 1990, we have the historical event of the United Nations ratifying the Convention on the Rights of the Child. Included in the document was Article 31 on Leisure,

Play and Culture: "Children have the right to relax and play, and to join in a wide range of cultural, artistic and other recreational activities."[3] The obvious question that comes to mind is what is so important about play?

Most psychologists and educators would agree that play allows children to learn new skills in a safe environment. Through mental and physical activities of play, children learn how to communicate with others, how to control their own emotions, and how to build patience and resilience. Through play, children learn how to be a hero and how to be a great teammate. Now, re-read the last three sentences replacing the word "children" with "adults." It may sound awkward at first, but there is an important question that follows. Let's ask ourselves are we any better at communicating with others, controlling our emotions, being a leader or a team player than we were five or ten years ago?

The "you can't teach an old dog new tricks" fallacy has proliferated much of Western popular culture, including the corporate world. Ignoring the overwhelming amount of research and personal stories pointing to the contrary, advancing in age is still associated with the inability of an individual to change the ways of communicating, while getting grumpier. With the entrance of younger employees, the "I am the boss" leadership style does not promote much of a genuine, engaged team.

The first step towards the solution is to realize that people are not dogs and that our brain is a bit more complex. In fact, advances in neuroscience have shown that we can continue learning way beyond our high school and college days. The second step is to continue with play as the means to learn new skills with the minimal risk to an organization should the player stumble. I remember going through my own corporate training at a large regional bank. It included groups of new employees role-playing customer service situations, learning to trust each other by doing "trust falls," breaking into teams and competing for gold stars as if we were back in grade school. We can all adopt the mentality of looking for opportunities to learn through play whether at work or at home. Here are some ideas:

- Telling a co-worker a joke

- Going on a bike ride with children or a partner, or

- Playing fetch with a dog.

The benefits of play include stress reduction and improvements in brain function. If we could incorporate a little play time in our busy work schedules (especially during stressful times at work), imagine the possibilities! Why not take a few minutes and creatively disrupt the negativity that may have been a result of a heated exchange with a customer, supplier, supervisor, subordinate, or a teammate, with a brisk walk or a short funny video? I have conducted many experiments where I would deliberately laugh and, eventually, all around me would start laughing. Laughing is just as contagious as negative talk.

Laughter Clubs, also known as Laughter Yoga, were popularized by Indian physician Madan Kataria, who wrote about the benefits of laughter in his 2002 book *Laugh For No Reason*. While the research is limited to a few studies, it does point out the improvement in cardiovascular health, the elevated pain thresholds, and a better overall mood. Additionally, the endorphins produced during voluntary laughter make it easier for individuals to connect and bond.

Laughter Clubs have turned out to be serious business. Over the years, around 2,500 groups formed all over the world and included locations in India, United Kingdom, Germany, Sweden, Norway, Denmark, Canada, and the United States. Today, the acceptance of humor and laughter can be found inside the workplace, among managers of all levels.

Theatrical play, or acting on stage, brings another dimension to cognitive studies that had not even started until the late 1990s. The reason for the delay was technological. The advances in MRI technology, such as functional MRIs (fMRI), made it possible for scientists to study various areas of the brain in more detail. In their writing on *Cognitive Studies, Theatre, and Performance*, Rhonda Blair and John Lutterbie talk about how understanding the cognitive science that explains perception, behaviors, emotions, and feelings we experience in everyday life, can be applied in understanding cognition during a pretend play of acting.[4] With many acknowledgments to possible limitations, misinterpretations, and other limiting conditions, the article still provides enough to support the importance of acting as an ultimate exercise in empathy. Provided by fMRI technology, the ability to imagine or to mirror Actions of others was tracked down to clusters of neurons. Much more work is still ahead as the human brain is a complex subject to study. On a less scientific note, we all heard some kind of variation of the expression "If you want to be one, you better start acting like one!" That is an invitation to learn about one's Beliefs through one's Actions.

Action movies are another great area to explore. When children and adults are describing their favorite heroes, they use more verbs and fewer titles. Superman saves the day. Batman protects Gotham City. The Actions of the heroes reveal the Values that they represent. Let's try an exercise. According to Inc. Magazine, these are the "important traits," let's call them Values, of highly effective leaders. Listed in Figure 3.2 are the Leadership Values. Try to come up with Action verbs or short expressions that would describe the behaviors that would clearly connect to the Values in the right column. Write your answers in the left column. How easy was that? Did you have to recall a certain individual(s) acting certain way to help with the exercise? Who were they?

Fig. 3.2

Leardership Actions	Leadership Values
	Inspiring Action
	Optimism
	Integrity
	Being Supportive
	Confidence
	Communication
	Descisivness

I have conducted the above exercise with groups of small business owners at a local chamber of commerce and was impressed with the range of possible Actions from a playful "smile" to a more serious "listen." As the group members, many of them successful entrepreneurs, were sharing their thoughts, I would take notes. Later, I would go over the list of Actions and, mentally, assess my own level. What a humbling experience that was!

Young professionals will often adopt imitation as the means to learn, grow, and move up the career ladder. Below are several excerpts from the book *Liar's Poker* that describes how Michael Lewis, the author, who eventually became a successful bond trader at Salomon Brothers, acquired the mindset, or used Beliefs and Values, through an Action of imitation.

"I had the ability to imitate. It enabled me to get inside the brain of another person. To learn how to make smart noises about money, I studied the two best Salomon salesmen I knew... My training amounted to absorbing and synthesizing their attitudes and skills.

My job was a matter of learning to think and sound like a money spinner. Thinking and sounding like Alexander was the next best thing to being genuinely talented which I wasn't. So I listened to the master and repeated what I heard, as in kung fu. It reminded me of learning a foreign language. It all seems strange at first. Then, one day, you catch yourself thinking in the language. Suddenly words you never realized you knew are at your disposal. Finally, you dream in the language." [5]

Michael Lewis's use of learning a foreign language as a metaphor for learning a new trade's terminology and concepts rings true with me. I too had to learn banking jargon, but not before I attained college level proficiency in English. Proper pronunciation required hours of repetition to train the muscles to move in a new way. Over time, muscle memory made it easier to speak and the thought process no longer required translating from a native tongue.

Muscle memory, or consolidation of specific motor tasks into memory through repetition, is not a memory stored in muscles, but an automatic neural pathway inside the brain that is developed by deliberate physical actions. After enough repetitions, the "memory" will move the muscles with a high degree of consistency. That's how we learned to crawl, walk, and run. The process takes time. That's why professional performance in sports or music, for instance, takes years to develop and a lifetime to perfect. The seeming ease of a piano performer or a figure skater is possible because difficult parts of the performance are run on "autopilot" by one part of the brain – mostly the cerebellum, allowing the other parts of the frontal lobe to function with less stress associated with the performance itself. This allows multitasking of interacting with an audience while exhibiting motor skills that take many years to master.

Great philosophers of the past were not familiar with neuroscience and there was no technology that would allow them to observe the connection between the body, mind, and soul as a collection of scientific data. However, they had some great insights as they observed human behavior. One of these philosophers was Plato. Around 380 BC he wrote *Republic*, a pretend dialog with Socrates. Just read the passage below from Book III, the relevance of which to the modern day is simply phenomenal:

"The very exercises and tolls which he undergoes are intended to stimulate the spirited element of his natures, and not to increase his strength; he will not, like common athletes, use exercise and regiment to develop muscles.

Very right, he [Socrates] said.

Neither are the two arts of music and gymnastics really designed, as is often supposed, the one for the training of the soul, the other for the training of the body.

What then is the real object of them?

I believe, I said, that the teachers of both have in view chiefly the improvement of the soul.

How can it be? He asked.

Did you never observe, I said, the effect on the mind itself the exclusive devotion to gymnastics, or the opposite effect on an exclusive devotion to music?

In what way shown? He said.

The one producing a temper of hardness and ferocity, the other of softness and effeminacy, I replied.

Yes, he said, I am quite aware that the mere athlete becomes too much of a savage, and that the mere musician is melted and softened beyond what is good for him.

Yet surely, I said, the ferocity only comes from spirit, which, if rightly educated, would give courage, but, if too much indulged, will turn to softness, but, if educated rightly, will be gentle and moderate.

True."

Sometimes, learning through play requires interaction with an environment that is unique and specific to learning objectives. When the real-life situation is not readily available for a large number of learners or the stakes are simply too high to allow for mistakes, a different type of play is used. Simulation, among many other functions, allows a safe interaction between an individual and various types of environments. The objective of these interactions is to learn and master new skills necessary to consistently deliver the desired outcomes. Figure 3.3 lists some of the fields that employ simulation.

Fig. 3.3

Automotive	Equipment	Robotics
Biomechanics	Finance	Production
Business	Flight	Satellite Navigation
Communication	Manufacturing	Space
Emergency Response	Marine	Sports
Engineering	Military	Weather

While some of the simulation equipment, such as a flight simulator, may sound like an exciting idea to try, it is not built for entertainment. Many hours of various routines will have to be logged before a new pilot is entrusted with real planes and with the lives of others. New skills through cognition will ultimately change certain Beliefs and Values of a new pilot. Perhaps, it will be a stronger appreciation for discipline, attention for details, and teamwork.

Nuances of one's environment will add new dimensions to core Beliefs. Think about a person, who takes a course for several years and becomes a military pilot. Are their values different from a commercial pilot? Why? Thinking this through will reveal certain Actions, like flying combat missions, which will showcase the incremental difference in Values of a military pilot compared to Values of a commercial pilot. I suspect that a military pilot might value peace a bit stronger.

Coaching can be compared to a simulation. During a coaching session, the coach will create a coaching space that will exist only in the minds of a coach and a client. Within this space, anything can be examined and tried safely. In some way, this resembles a simulator where one's memories, experiences, and imagination will fill the space with a variety of scenarios, objects, and ideas. While this may sound like a brain in a vat, a coaching space is a unique structure that allows for time and cost effective discovery of current states of affairs, their causes, and the various ways to move towards desired goals.

The coaching space, if a virtual simulator, is no substitute for the actions taken in reality. I keep saying to those who are new to coaching that the real magic happens in-between the sessions. That's when a client executes on the agreed-upon plan of actions and brings back newly acquired knowledge to the coaching space for further discussion.

I prefer to keep weekly meetings. That is an optimal amount of time to "try on" a new course of Action and to remember the outcomes, either desired or not. During the coaching session that follows, all the details of the prior week's experiences will be tested for relevance and value in the context of the entire Model and cataloged accordingly.

Did you know that on average, a car has 30,000 parts? That is at the level of a single screw. Even at the larger, component level, on average, a car has about 2,000 component parts. If a narrower goal of coaching is to modify one's behavior, each newly adopted approach can be compared to a part of a new car. Given time and effort, an old rusty clunker can be transformed into a sleek hot rod!

Chapter Summary.

Beliefs and Actions have a complex, two-way relationship. The information is constantly traveling from one Wheel to another to either reinforce or to make changes of various magnitudes.

Going in the direction from Values and Beliefs to Actions, we often contemplate and filter our Actions by calling upon three types of reasons:

- Normative = Actions that are expected of us by others.

- Motivational = Actions that we expect from ourselves.

- Explanatory = Actions that we expected to occur based on facts.

These reasons are always running in the background and unless we take the time to think, we may not be aware of what drives us to make certain important decisions.

Going from Actions to Beliefs and Values, the cognition process allows us to learn by doing. Though not specifically identified in the Model, cognition is always involved in a learning process. The Actions below were explored as inputs for cognition:

- Play – children and adults learn through it.

- Imitation – a way to learn how to think like someone else.

- Simulation – an artificial environment where new skills can be developed safely and cost effectively. Coaching space can be looked at as a simulation that allows for a transformation process to take place.

Chapter Four: Relationship Between Wheels of Actions and Measurements.

As we have already seen in Chapter One, measuring progress towards the achievement of Goals is challenging. To simplify this task, society has created standards for various socio-economic classes. These standards apply to all areas of life including health, wealth, status, and even longevity. For example, the standards applied to a slave would be quite different than those applied to a royal. Achieving an undisputed success for a Roman slave could have been as simple as living to see his or her twentieth birthday considering the average recorded age at death was 17-and-a-half years old.[1]

Dwelling on the history a bit more, it is important to understand that in the not so distant past, most did not know how to read or write. The chart below depicts the dynamics of world literacy for the past 200 years.[2]

Figure 5.1. **World development of literacy and attainment of at least basic education, 1820-2010**

Percentage of population aged over 15 literate or enrolled in formal education

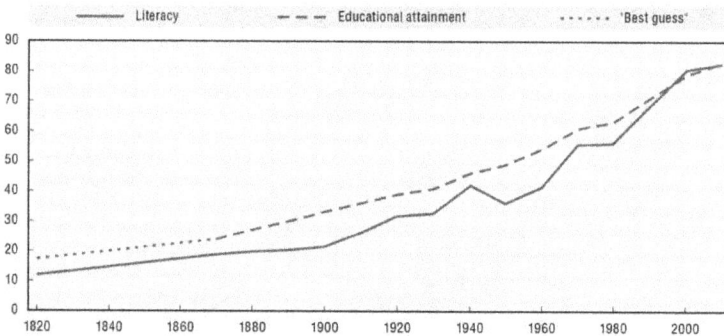

Note: For an assessment of data quality, see Table 5.2.
Source: Clio-Infra, www.clio-infra.eu.

StatLink ⬛ http://dx.doi.org/10.1787/888933095666

Today, due to the advances in computer and information technologies, we have more opportunities to acquire knowledge and skills than ever before. At the same time, the type of information that is found on the Internet is not free of self-serving biases, and, unless we know exactly what we are looking for in the first place, we could be easily misled by content from sponsored messages or some higher-ranked website that appears on the first page of our search.

Once a near 100% literacy rate was achieved, it provided an equal opportunity for those who are seeking information as well as for those who are providing the information. Being an information seeker, I spend a considerable amount of time online. Recently, I have started noticing a particular type of content. At first, I did not see a connection to Measurement. Then, the connection appeared. The content I am talking about is quotes.

This is a screenshot I took on October 5, 2016.

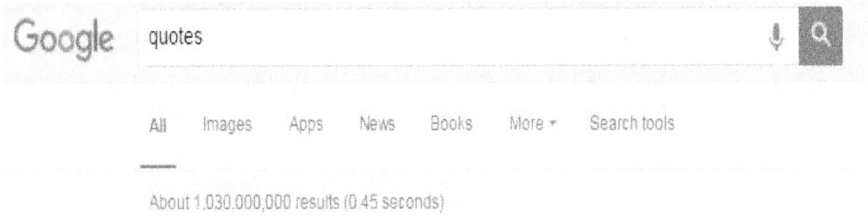

Google quotes 🎤 🔍

All   Images   Apps   News   Books   More ▾   Search tools

About 1,030,000,000 results (0.45 seconds)

Over a billion search results in less than half a second! When I selected the "Images" result tab, this is what a part of my screen looked like:

This is the reality we are facing. Each of the quotes contains certain perspectives uttered by great thinkers, dead or alive. Each quote, when read separately, could be helpful if put to practice. However, if we are to read twenty or thirty quotes together and try to make sense of them collectively, then we would start to see some contradictions.

My favorite contradiction has to do with two groups of quotes. The first group espouses "hard work" and the second espouses "working smart." The words "hard" and "smart" are loaded with judgment regarding our work. The opposite of working hard is being lazy, and the opposite of working smart is being stupid. Therefore, the work we do would fall on this imaginary scale that measures how hard or smart we work. It must have been a period of a week or two when it seemed the only quotes that came through my social media feed were about either hard work or working smart. Overwhelmed with self-inflicted judgments I wrote: "If I am working smart, I am lazy, if I am working hard, I am stupid. If I knew how, I would be working SHMARDT!"

How do you measure hard? How do you measure smart? It is all situational, and using hours worked, as a possible way of measurement, is misleading. Let's admit it, we can all be better time managers. We can all be better at saying "no" to the irresistible time wasting activities. Moreover, staying focused on the task at hand is the key. Working hard is also smart if you can focus on 20 minutes of uninterrupted work. Working hard is smart if in 20 minutes you can accomplish an hour's worth of work because you were able to avoid distractions. At the same time, it is hard to work smart because of competing priorities. You may wonder if there is a solution. Yes, there is. The solution is a conscious effort to improve focus and the ability to withstand the instant gratification that comes from unproductive or low-priority activities. They can never be completely eliminated, but they can be reduced. For instance, if you cut the time you are watching TV during the work week from 90 minutes a day to 60 minutes, you would save 150 minutes – or two and a half hours each week. That's over eight hours a month! Imagine what can be done during those hours and how you will feel about yourself accomplishing more of what you truly want to accomplish.

There is a constant, two-way relationship between the Wheels of Measurements and Actions. Working hard and smart are examples of some typical small judgement calls that, if heard enough times, may make you feel less confident in your abilities. If gone unchecked, small judgments can become heavy self-judgments and influence the way you measure yourself.

Just like we can benefit from a high-intensity 30 minute workout, we can also benefit from highly focused work performed in shorter amounts of time. Additionally, we can change the way we think about working hard, smart, or any other intangible measurements that are intertwined in quotes. Keep your focus on your commitments as long as you can. Let your Actions be a leader and you'll be happier with the results.

The ambiguity of measuring an intangible world, so well depicted by quotes, is not an issue when it comes to measuring economic growth. Since the 1950s, Gross National Product (GNP) and Gross Domestic Product (GDP) became the main measurements of economic well-being for countries. The post-World War II global economy was given this new performance measurement tool to help quickly assess economic growth. Simply put, GDP takes monetary values of all the goods and services produced in a given period and compares that to a prior period's values to determine either growth or decline. Additionally, the GDP of one country is compared to the GDP of other countries. To account for population size, a per capita GDP is also used.

Economic prosperity, as expressed by the size of overall or, per capita production, is usually tied to a general well-being of the country and its population. Nevertheless, this logic does not always hold true. Since 2012, a handful of economists have been publishing World Happiness Reports. Figure 4.1 lists the top fifteen countries based on overall GDP, a per capita GDP, and their happiness ranking.[3]

Fig. 4.1

	2016	2015	2016
	GDP overall	GDP per capita (IMF)	Ranking of Happiness
1	United States	Qatar	Denmark
2	China	Luxembourg	Switzerland
3	Japan	Singapore	Iceland
4	Germany	Brunei	Norway
5	United Kingdom	Kuwait	Finland
6	France	Norway	Canada
7	India	United Arab Emirates	Netherlands
8	Italy	Ireland	New Zealand
9	Brazil	San Marino	Australia
10	Canada	Switzerland	Sweden
11	Korea	United States	Israel
12	Spain	Saudi Arabia	Austria
13	Australia	Netherlands	United States
14	Russia	Bahrain	Costa Rica
15	Mexico	Sweden	Puerto Rico

If the size of the economy or per capita production do not necessary equate to happiness, what are some of the factors that do? According to the World Happiness Report, these are the other important factors:

- Social support

- Healthy life expectancy

- Freedom to make life choices

- Generosity

- Perceptions of corruption

- Dystopia

During the 2016 World Economic Forum in Davos, the Nobel Prize winning economist Joseph Stiglitz said: "What we measure informs what we do. And if we're measuring the wrong thing, we're going to do the wrong thing."[4] This was said regarding a growing concern that traditional methods for measuring the economy and growth are no longer relevant. Traditional methods of economic measurements miss activities at home, like housekeeping and time spent with children. GDP is just the value of things with total disregard of what these things are and what technology was used to make them.

So far we have covered the relationship between Measurements and Actions Wheels at an individual level as well as at the level of the global economy. In both cases, we saw that what we measure and how we measure is important and will influence the way we act, either as individuals or as a global marketplace.

Somewhere in between an individual and the global marketplace there is a middle level made up of groups of people. Next, we are going to look at some of the Measurements and Actions that are common for that level. Our focus will be on teams and families.

Teams.

People have always teamed up to perform tasks that would be hard or impossible to perform by a single person. Big-game hunting, building homes, and caravan travel are some of the examples of team activities that have been around for a long time. Measuring performance of these teams used to be simple. An animal killed, a house built, or a destination reached signified a team's successful performance.

The Industrial Age brought the factors of time and cost to the measurement matrix. Successful performance was redefined to include projects completed on time and within budget. In the later part of the 20th Century, the "what gets measured gets done" maxim attributed to Peter Drucker, Tom Peters, and Edwards Deming took hold. Organizations that rely on teams embraced performance measurement for the decades to come. Arguably, volume and the quality of output were the first factors to be measured. While these factors are important to the company's bottom line, the way to increase both is to look at certain characteristics that high performing teams are exhibiting. Usually, these characteristics will include:

- Group size

- Synergy

- Cohesiveness

- Vision

- Leadership

Group size depends on the type of problems they are to solve. Smaller groups of three to five members will tend to reach consensus and move forward faster solving a less complex problem, while larger groups of seven to twelve may be required to solve a more complex problem.

Synergy, or a collective output that is greater than a sum of individual outputs, is achieved when each member is carefully considered. The reason for careful consideration is that synergy can be either positive or negative. In case of a negative synergy, the collective output will be less than the sum of individual outputs.

Cohesiveness is stronger when members align their individual goals to the team's goal, trust one another, and have confidence in each other's abilities. At the same time, the focus of a cohesive team should be the process of achieving team goals.

The overarching theme that connects team goals is team vision. Usually expressed as a vision statement, vision is the "why" of team goals and actions. Vision inspires, motivates, and connects the present with the future. Writing a mission statement is a great exercise in leadership.

Great teams are impossible without leadership. The size of the team, characteristics of the individual members, and the team's goals will define right leadership approach.

***

Can you think of a case where the contribution of an individual team member would be completely disregarded? It is hard to imagine, isn't it? Sports fans involved in fantasy sports know the stats of their favorite teams and their favorite players so well that they're willing to risk real money as they trade players and build their teams.

Teams in professional arenas other than sports are also measured with individual performance considerations in mind: for instance, sales goals for a sales manager. That said, making decisions based on an individual's output alone can be misleading. A person with the lowest output may be contributing to the team in ways not being measured. For instance, the person may be keeping the morale up, or coming up with cost saving ideas, or mentoring new team members. Provided that these activities are not part of the person's job description, these are all value-added contributions to the team. These Actions, while not being measured by the standard volume/quality matrix, are still adding value to the team. On the flip side, a person's volume/quality numbers could be high but their arrogant attitude and pushy behavior may be contributing to a toxic environment. Just like the GDP misses out on contributions provided by non-working members, i.e. stay at home parents, it is also possible to overlook Actions that contribute to the well-being of team because these Actions may not be visible through traditional Measurements.

Family.

We have already touched on the importance of family in forming our Beliefs and Values. Part of that process includes opportunities for families to work as a team. These opportunities include raising children and providing them with opportunities to learn as much as they can about life in the protected environment of their home. The "it takes a village to raise a child" proverb illustrates the kind of effort required to support individual growth and to provide a space to celebrate or to grieve, depending on life's circumstances. Today, it is harder to find a "village" of supportive adults. Instead, a higher emphasis has been placed on creating or seeking alternative structures of support. Because our individual needs vary, some of us may find that support at a meetup group or at a networking event. Others may be better served by engaging a professional consultant. However, there is no substitute for the love and care that is coming from parents or other family members.

How can we measure success or happiness of a family? What are some of the Measurements at play? In my research, I've come across a very interesting work that was done at the turn of the 20th Century by an Australian group of social scientists titled "Indicators of Social and Family Functioning".[5] The reason I've included the selected parts below is threefold. First, to simply show the selection of the five key factors that went into the creation of the questionnaire that follows. Second is to show the depth of each factor. Finally, to bring awareness of the actionable items these five factors of measurement were designed to reveal. Well thought out Measurements lead to great

Actions. The final disclaimer is that the focus of the report and the questionnaire was the well-being of children.

1. Five key factors of social and family functioning:

- Time – measured in terms of quality and quantity and includes both a number of hours of parental or paid help as well as the particular activities e.g. doing homework, reading together with a child, or recreational activities.

- Income – measured mostly and preferably in terms of annual income. The idea is that the higher the income, the more the other factors can be employed. Proxy or indirect measurements sometimes used include educational level and occupation. As family members may lose employment, these proxies are used as predictors of income level and stability.

- Human Capital – measures educational level, experience, and employment status of caregivers other than parents. Also, Human Capital refers to the caregiver's knowledge, beliefs, attitudes, values, and traditions towards parenting and family life.

- Psychological Capital – questions in this category measure the level of stress associated with life events. The term itself, however, refers to a parents' mental health, level of family cohesion, and the level of emotional stress and violence within the family.

- Social Capital – concerns with interactions within groups of people living in close proximity, e.g. neighborhoods. Qualities important to this concept include trust, civic involvement, social engagement, and reciprocity. Questions in this category measure these qualities as a way access the overall depth of social capital.

2. The depth of factors. Using social capital as an example, below is a list of considerations that funnel into the social capital factor of the overall study.

- Participation in local community

- Proactivity in a social context

- Feelings of trust and safety

- Neighborhood connections

- Neighborhood violence and crimes

- Family and friends connections

- Tolerance of diversity

- Social or cultural discrimination

- Value of Life

- Work connections

- Measures of school and classroom characteristics (curriculum, student body demographics)

- Sense of neighborhood

- Sense of community

- Social participation in sports, clubs, groups

- Civic participation in community of school activities

- Social Trust

- Availability of support services

- Philanthropy

3. The magnitude of specific problems the Measurements are designed to reveal in terms of children's developmental health.

- Physical Health

  Low birth weight / premature birth

  Maternal depression

  Sudden Infant Death Syndrome

  Unintentional injury

  Failure to thrive

- Developmental and Learning

  Attention problems (irritability, inattention, impulsivity)

  Aggression

  Delinquency

  Social problems

  Emotional problems (anxiety, depression, suicidal ideation / completion)

- Risk Behaviors

  Substance use (alcohol, smoking, illicit drugs)

  Eating disorders

  Early sexual activity

  Teenage parenting

- Academic Outcomes

  Truancy

  Early school leaving

  Poor academic achievement

  Low participation in school activities

  Attachment to a deviant peer group

  Alienation

- Social Outcomes

  Family breakdowns

  Child abuse and neglect

  Children in institutions

  Children in care

  Detached youth

  Criminal behavior

As we can see, Measurements of social environments are used to predict some undesirable outcomes or Actions.

The Measurements that were developed in this study are not the reflection of cultural norms that are only relevant to Australian society. Just by glancing at the long list of references, we can see names of experts representing European and North American institutions. The development of the economies in many countries, while providing opportunities to increase the standard of living, came at a price of shrinking psychological, social, and, to some degree, human capital.

We have started Chapter Four at an individual level, jumped to a macro level, zoomed into team and family levels in order to discover the complexity of Measurements on each level.

Measurements either seemed too ambiguous or too narrow, or take a lot of work to put together. The "so what?" that some of you may still have brings us back to an individual level and to some Actions that, perhaps, we have not considered or deemed as useless. The reason we may not have considered certain Actions may be due to lack of awareness that these opportunities exist. The reason we may deem some Actions useless is either due to prior experiences or due to rationalization.

When we look at a broader picture of the world, we often feel like we can do very little to change it. Our mind makes that statement and adds some negative connotations to it. Taking it one step further, the statement gets filed away into a Beliefs Wheel and becomes part of an upgrade to our operating system. However, feeling powerless is not a true lack of power. If we are psychically and mentally capable individuals of adult age, living in a civilized world, we do have opportunities to express our thoughts and contribute to various causes. We can apply ourselves at home, school, work, and in various interest groups.

Often in our travels, we come across a city or a town that we fall in love with. We admire the cleanliness of the streets and the friendliness of people. At that moment we do not think about all the effort that is behind what meets the eye. We tend to take it for granted. Yet, it is the Actions of the people that live and work there that result in clean streets and other memorable and picture-worthy attributes. The good news is that we do have the power to make places we live and work look like the places we visit as tourists.

Any new city development incorporates a designing stage. A new park or a building or a large improvement project first comes into existence in a form of artistic rendering. Much like a designer or an architect, we can create a visual of the desired outcomes of our Actions and, as we move towards them, we should periodically engage Measurements so that we know where we are. To illustrate this further, below is an excerpt from an executive coaching session where a coaching tool called "Old House – New House" was utilized. In this case, the Coach knew that her client was in the process of building a new house and used that knowledge to ask some powerful questions.[6]

Coach: So, did you see many floor plans recently?
Coachee: Tons of them! You know, our house is being built on a hillside, and so we had to figure out how to ensure sufficient room while at the same time not having to climb the stairs all the time.
Coach: I see. Would you be interested in using floor plans to identify your coaching objective?
Coachee: My boss didn't mention that you were also offering architectural services. If I had known, I would have asked for a quotation, he said with laughter. But sure, let's give it a try.
Coach: So imagine that you have a two-story house where the first floor is your personal life and the second floor is your professional life.
Coachee: Wait, that's not good!
Coach: Why?
Coachee: Because a house would not be statically strong with twenty square feet downstairs and a second floor that is a thousand square feet.
Coach: Are you suggesting that there is an imbalance between your work and your personal life?
Coachee: We haven't even started drawing, and you have already identified the objective? That was rather quick since we haven't even been talking for seven minutes.
Coach: It must have been just a coincidence, a stroke of luck. But let's examine this in greater detail. If you can already think along these lines, then tell me presently how large is the children's room, the bedroom where you sleep with your wife, and the living room where you entertain friends and family?
Coachee: OK, so this was not simply a lucky coincidence, but it is really a good tool. Funny you should ask, because we do have a bedroom in our apartment, which is approximately 12 square

meters, but in reality it's zero. One of the reasons why we embarked on this construction project is that our three children currently share a 20-square-meter room and in the new house each will have a 15-square-meter room. However, I presently devote enough time to them; in other words their share would not have to be modified as they demand and obtain what they need, but that is not the case with my wife. Would it be possible to really think out of the box here?

Coach: Absolutely, if we were to do it somewhere, this is it!

Coachee: Can I draw a balcony?

Coach: Of course, if that's what you would like…

Coachee: Very much so! And I will immediately remove my mother-in-law from our living room!

Coach: Can I summarize the past two minutes?

Coachee: (nods)

Coach: If I understood correctly, you have a problem balancing your professional and personal lives. However, this is not a classic scenario where your children hardly know you. Rather, it is you and your wife who do not have enough time for each other. Your other problem is that your mother-in-law is accorded too large of a role in the family.

Coachee: Yes! I would never have thought that a coach, being an outsider, would be able to see things so clearly.

Coach: With respect to the two issues, the latter (the one concerning your mother-in-law) is clearly a life coaching issue, whereas with the former, although it is also related to your lifestyle, has its origins in your work. As you know, I am an executive coach, and your company is paying me to help you become a more successful leader, and therefore, if you also agree, we should primarily focus on this issue.

Coachee: I agree. I will solve the problem with my mother-in-law on my own.

Coach: This floor plan is a coaching tool which helps us define the objectives, but not find the solution. Therefore, let me ask you now, taking into account all of this, to make a drawing of your current home and the home of your dreams.

Coachee: (busy drawing)

Coach: OK, so as I can see in your current "living space," nearly 80% is devoted to work and 20% to your personal life, out of which 18% belongs to your children, 2% to sports and 0% each to your friends and your wife. Then, in the new house, you would like to devote 50% to work, 18% to your children (meaning no change), also 18% to your wife, and 7% each to sports and friends. If this house was to be achieved at the end of the coaching process, would you consider it a success?

Coachee: Yes.

Coach: So, let's get down to business, shall we?

Coachee: Sure. Just a second. As I understand, this tool was used for defining the objective of the coaching, so can we stay with it a little longer?

Coach: OK. What would you like to do?

Coachee: I think we could make progress if I could break down the 80% devoted to work in the same way I did with my personal life. That way, I would not only see that I would like to go from 80% to 50%, but also what the 30% to be cut would be comprised of. We could then take another step and determine how it could be reduced. Could we do that?

Coach: Of course! Coaching is all about helping you.

Coachee: If I divide up my work on the basis of time devoted to various tasks, I would say that out of the 80% approximately,
40% is spent attending pointless meetings,
5% in productive meetings,
5% in strategic tasks that cannot be delegated,
20% on paperwork,
10% listening to and helping my employees speak their mind…

Coach: I see. And what would it look like in an ideal world?

Coachee: Yes, I can see the solution already! If I could cut back the time spent at pointless meetings to 10%, then it would leave me with exactly the needed 30% to solve my problems.

Coach: In which percentage of the cases do you realize this in the first five minutes, and how often is it that you conclude that a meeting is pointless only afterwards?

Coachee: In the majority of cases, when I look at the list of participants and the agenda, I know already that there is no real point in being there, but I usually go nevertheless. I always find out by the end of the fifth minute at the latest; I never realize that afterwards.

Coach: Alright. What are your options?

Coachee: I could avoid attending the meetings, or I could stand up and leave.

Coach: Which one is more difficult for you?

Coachee: Well, I guess it's harder to stand up and leave once you are already there.

Coach: Try the following: Next week, choose one meeting that you will not attend. Then, the week after, choose three, and on week three, either cancel all meetings that you consider to be pointless for attendance purposes or send someone else in your place.

Coachee: This homework will be a significant challenge, but I'd like to try it and see whether the company will collapse...

***

As we have seen thus far, measuring certain aspects of various environments has its challenges. We need to know what we are measuring and why. We also have to have the right tools for the job. The combination of what, why, and how will help create a good measurement and analytical tool. At the same time, if the incoming information or input is not valid, the output will not be useful. This leads to the question: "What are the valid sources of information?"

In terms of the topics of life coaching, the information we use for measurements of actions often includes thoughts, feelings, and emotions. For instance, in measuring how effective a workout is, not only do we look at the number of calories burned and the amount of weight lost, but we also may add a statement like "and it made me feel great!" In an effort to promote gym membership, marketers often employ a softer side and use words like "confidence" and "looks." The images inside the gym often portray the emotions of happiness or a mental state of calmness. Are these valid factors to a successful workout and, if so, why?

Think about advertisements for jewelry, restaurants, and travel destinations. Their success depends on our level of spending that cannot be rationalized by logic alone. A promise of a deeper relationship, a positive experience, and long lasting memories are all appealing to our emotions and the emotions of those who will be sharing the experience with us. As we leave our comments on review sites like Yelp, for instance, we often include words like "happy," "stunning," and "love." In doing so we add an emotional aspect to our measurement of an experience. Even though it is called a review, we are asked to rank it by giving it up to five stars. Ranking is a comparative measurement.

At this point, we may say that there are simply too many ways to measure things that are small, big, near, and far. It may seem that for every action, visible and not, there is already a way to measure it. It may even seem that the relationship between the Measurements and Actions Wheels is elusive, superficial, or non-existent. However, there is an overarching theme that is present in most, if not all, measurements of actions. Once we view all the actions in terms of it, it will reveal a whole new dimension to everything that we do, think, and experience emotionally. It is a dimension in its own right: it is Time.

Time.

While some scientists continue to argue whether or not time is part of a three-dimensional world, it is still an extremely useful measurement tool. The notion of time has been with us for thousands of years. Time enters our lives the minute we are born and stays with us for the rest of our lives. It is a part of our everyday vocabulary. We utilize the concept of time in our thinking and feeling. "It felt like time stopped" is a statement that contains both the concept of time as an Action and as a Measurement.

Think about the way we measure important things in life like success, significance, and wisdom. How does time factor in our individual discernment of our own actions or the actions of others? Is faster always better? What is the ideal time period in a current occupation before a career switch? Are we supposed to be wise by a certain age?

I suspect that if I was to receive answers from 10 individuals, I would get answers that would be slightly different. Some will ask me to clarify. This is exactly the reason why life coaching is designed to work with an individual's view of the world at that specific point in time. Every time the coach and the client meet, a client comes out of a coaching session with a few actionable items. The Actions take place during the time period between the sessions. It takes time for a client to establish the desired new habits. I have purposely overused the word "time" to drive home the point. The omnipresence of time is what makes it a metaphorical axle between the Wheels of Measurements and Actions.

MEASUREMENTS

ACTIONS

How can we measure the Four Wheel Alignment in our lives? An in-depth self-assessment would be one way, but it is not a part of this book. That said, the discussion of this chapter would be incomplete without at least a general framework. Please review Model, Figure 1.1, and take your time when answering the questions below. The answers may reveal some uneasiness in certain areas of your life due to the lack of the Four Wheels being in alignment with each other.

- What are some thoughts that keep you up at night?

- What are some thoughts that keep you distracted during the day?

- Do these thoughts come from the place of fear or love?

- Do these thoughts inspire you to act, to take on more, or do they make you want to stop and give up?

- Look around. Is this where you want to be? Why?

- Does the space you are in now define you?

- What do you do so well you could teach others?

- How do you motivate yourself?

- How do you choose what to focus on next?

- Are your shoulders relaxed? Is your back straight?

- What habits you are glad you have?

- What business or occupation would you pursue if there was no competition? Why?

- If money was no object, what car would you drive? Why?

- Thus far, what has been the best investment of your time?

Chapter Summary.

The relationship between the Wheels of Actions and Measurements may at first glance seem either too obvious or superficial. "Do-measure-do" or "measure-do-measure" concepts may seem too easy to comprehend. While easy to comprehend, the concepts are hard to implement. Focused work is hard, and working smart is even harder. Delivering consistent results and staying on top of your game, in addition to the constant Actions of effort, requires a process of Measurements. Choosing the right measurement tools and assumptions may also seem like shooting at a moving target blindfolded.

Have you ever engaged in watching people walk in parks, shopping malls, airports, or the busy streets of large cities? Have you observed the difference in speed and the various tactics to avoid collision with other pedestrians? If you have, chances are you have made some assumptions about these people based on their Actions. You have measured them against some internal references that placed them on a certain scale or range. As a quick exercise, mentally insert yourself among the others while keeping an outside perspective and apply the same Measurements. Would this change the way you walk, your facial expression, or how you interact with others?

Time is both our ally and our enemy. The finite nature of our lifespan, while frightening, is mobilizing. It takes time to grow up, learn the ways of the world, and then apply what we have learned to ourselves. Once we reach a point of maturity and the desire to take responsibility for our actions, the value of time goes up infinitely. There are simply too many opportunities to improve the outcomes of self-Measurements through Actions. Make them count, but save the counting for a later day.

Chapter Five: Relationship Between Wheels of Measurements and Goals.

SMART Refresher.

As we have seen in the previous chapter, Measurements of results of our Actions are designed with outcomes in mind. In terms of the Model, the desired outcomes are located in the Wheel of Goals. Let's quickly review SMART criteria for setting personal Goals, as depicted in Figure 1.4. I will use a personal example as a refresher.

When I came up with the goal to write this book, I first ran it through SMART criteria for setting personal Goals. Here are the results:

Stretchable. *Will the Goal help me learn and grow?* Yes, I am learning a lot as I write each chapter. I do my own research and only about 20% of the material that I've reviewed is included in this book. Another 10% I anticipate using in the future for articles, video blogs, or in-person presentations.

Memorable. *Will I remember what my goal is?* Yes, I am using a dry erase board to help keep myself on track throughout the writing and editing process. I also keep a binder of reference materials up on my desk as a visual reminder. To stay focused I need all the help I can get.

Aligned – *Why am I pursuing the Goal?* My "why" is that I believe in sharing in a way that adds value. Books that I have read helped me to become the person I am today. Writing this book is my way to pay what I have learned forward.

Resourced – *Am I willing to commit resources?* This was the first question I answered with a definitive "yes" as I understood that writing a book is a project. I have also learned that most projects take more time and will cost more than indicated on the original estimates. The worst case scenario is that this book may not sell enough copies to recoup the investment, and I will have to make peace with the fact.

Taskable – *How will I achieve my Goal?* The answer to that is twofold. First, I took the time to create a chapter plan. Second, I am focusing on one chapter at a time. Sometimes, finding time to write is challenging. Yet, I am avoiding adding unnecessary stress by not setting deadlines.

Unlike the original SMART criteria, I don't have a Measurable unit for M. As a society, we are already preoccupied with scoring, reviewing, ranking, and judging. All these activities are variations of Measurements. Browsing through social media profiles, I often come across personal profiles that boast rankings of "#1" or "Top 1%." Usually, these rankings mean that a person sold a lot of goods or services in a given year. Sounds a lot like a "personal GDP," doesn't it? Just like in the case of a country's GDP, volume is a quantitative measure. As such, it encourages a certain type of thinking and behavior. Both are more transactional in nature. Such thinking and behavior often leave little time to develop deep relationships with clients and consumers. The beauty of being #1 in volume is only skin deep.

Going back to the SMART criteria for setting personal goals, each letter can offer an insight that more than compensates for not having a measurable M unit. As we try to answer the questions below, we will engage in thinking that helps to measure the "smartness" level of the goal, as defined by SMART and, to some extent, the progress made towards the goal.

Stretchable – What is there to learn? What area of knowledge or skill are you trying to grow? Where else can you apply the new knowledge or skills? Who else can benefit from that?

Memorable – Why it is important to remember? What or who will remind you? Once reminded, how likely are you to say "thank you?"

Aligned – Why am I doing it? What Beliefs and Values are motivating me? What am I trying to prove and to whom?

Resourced – How much time have you given? How do you know if it is enough or too much? What is the total cost? How can you turn the costs into investment? Can you afford to fail?

Taskable – What is the first step? What do you need to know to take the next step? Where can I get that information?

SMART Goals require smart Measurement tools.

If the outcomes are part of the Goals Wheel, what role is left for the Measurements Wheel in producing the desired outcome? A helpful way of thinking about the Measurement Wheel is to think of it as a tool. It can provide information about physical properties of objects and living things. It can also provide information about behaviors of people. If you could know anything about the behavior of others or yourself, what would that be? Remember, your Actions will either move you closer to your Goals or move you away from them. Considering the fact that the unplanned and the unforeseen can and do show up in our lives, it takes a considerable amount of time and effort to maintain forward momentum over a long period of time.

I frequently go to coffee shops to write while enjoying a fresh cup of java. The ambiance, music, and even the small talk I overhear while inline helps me to think more creatively. Being at the coffee shop as I am writing this very page got me thinking about Goals that coffee shops, as businesses, might have. Without much effort, I have identified revenues and profitability as typical financial goals any business would have.

Revenues increase as a business sells more and when the prices go up. The profitability goes up when the costs go down. On the other hand, these are not the only Goals that successful businesses have to accomplish.

Whether we are customers or service providers, we are engaged in an exchange that is often described as a *customer experience*. As customers, we want to have a great customer experience. As providers, we want our customers to have a great customer experience. The "greatness" of the experience is often correlated with higher revenues. Caution: a goal of providing great customer experience for the sake of higher revenues may not be the correct one. Today, market researchers are concerned with customer behaviors and attitudes that lead directly to new business and repeat business. In mature industries, the growth of revenue is challenged by competition and the need for new and repeat customers is crucial to maintaining the revenues, let alone to grow them.

Turns out, a desirable behavior and attitude of a customer are caused by exchanges with the provider. These exchanges may be a phone conversation initiated by a customer to resolve a service issue, or a face-to-face interaction as a prospect enters a sales office. Today, the exchanges often come in the form of social media marketing or targeted emails that inform potential or existing customers about new products and special offers. Measuring correlations between outcomes created by the service provider's actions on one side, and customer's behaviors and attitudes on the other side, is the focus of one marketing study we are going to take a look at next.

A comprehensive study conducted for a mortgage division of a major UK bank is summarized in the paragraphs below.[1] At the conclusion of the study, the researchers acknowledged any service-oriented companies with a high degree of customer interaction can benefit from their findings.

First, the study takes the reader from a general goal of quality to an operational level goal of a high-quality service experience. Second, the factors of a quality service experience were further defined as desirable outcomes and included loyalty, word of mouth, and customer satisfaction. See Figure 5.1 below.

Fig. 5.1

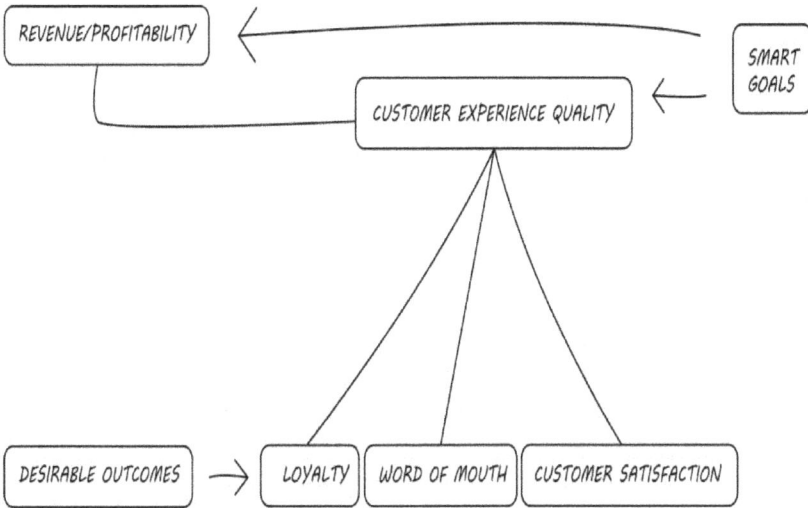

Loyalty was identified as one of the most important outcomes and was defined as "repurchase of the mortgage [product]."

Word of Mouth is a part of "longitudinal perspective when assessing [customers'] experiences that [customers] will believe that they had experience with a company even before they have bought something; this arises from advertising, promotion and word-of-mouth."

Customer Satisfaction, based on several studies, is "a more direct and quantifiable relationship empirically evident between customer satisfaction and outcomes. Satisfaction builds market share profitability, thus improving shareholder value, improves cash flow, whilst reducing risk, improves customers' commitment, deepens customers' relationship with the firm and enhances customers' propensity to pay a premium."

After the desired outcomes were identified, the real work was yet to be performed because measuring customer experience required a tool that was not available at the time. The creation of the tool involved a four stage process. The process involved interviewing customers, and four factors of the customer experience that could be used to predict outcomes emerged. Below are the four factors, or dimensions, as they referred to them.

1. **Product experience** – Customers' perception of having choices and the ability to compare offers. Interviewees often referred to the need to compare offers, even if they were from the same provider and differed merely in length of the mortgage, because it "gave them the feeling of having a choice," and without a choice they were unlikely to accept the offer "no matter how good it was."

2. **Outcome focus** – is associated with reducing customers' transaction costs, such as seeking out and qualifying new providers: "We just wanted to get the mortgage as soon as possible." Also, once a relationship is established, these goal-oriented past experiences build a habit despite the awareness of competitors' offers: "I know there are better offers, but why should I bother; here I know what I will get and it's straightforward."

3. **Moments-of-truth** – This dimension is characterized by that which is commonly known as moments-of-truth, emphasizing the importance of service recovery and flexibility when faced with unforeseen complications. This dimension also incorporates evaluations of bank employees' interpersonal skills connected to those moments-of-truths: "I was really upset about what

happened, but the way they [the bank] dealt with me, gave me the confidence that I had made the right decision in staying with them."

4. **Peace-of-mind** – This dimension includes statements associated strongly with the emotional aspects of service and is based upon the perceived expertise of the service provider and the guidance provided throughout the process. These attributes put customers at ease and increase confidence in the provider. In this research, customers link peace-of-mind with their relationship to the bank and express a preference for being dealt with as a valued customer rather than in a purely transactional way.

The tool or scale, as it was called in the study, measured correlation between the four factors of the customer experience and the desired outcomes. Figure 5.2 below summarizes the findings.

Fig. 5.2

	Desired Outcome		
Dimension	Loyalty	Word-of-Mouth	Customer Satisfaction
Product experience	0.09	0.04	0.10
Outcome focus	0.20	0.20	0.09
Moments-of-truth	0.13	0.09	0.04
Peace-of-mind	0.72	0.40	0.90

Does it come as a surprise that technical aspects of the customer experience, presented by the first three dimensions, combined, have less effect on the desired outcomes compared to a much more emotion-based peace-of-mind dimension? What other conclusions can you draw from Figure 5.2? How can you incorporate these findings in your personal or professional life?

The title of the above study must have been written by a life coach as it is written in the form of a question: *Are We Measuring the Right Things?* Indeed, are we? Taking a step back, the question becomes how do we know what to measure? Based on the study, it is obvious that the better the company is in the peace-of-mind dimension, the better the chances are that customers will be more loyal, satisfied, and that they will spread the word. While the study simply went back and calculated a correlation between customers' behaviors and attitudes after they interacted with employees in situations that fell into the four dimensions, some may have gotten the impression that an employee's behavior and attitudes caused the desired reaction on the customer's part. This brings us to a subject that for some of us needs either a refresher or clarification.

Correlation vs Causality.

The two basic mistakes that we make when we equate correlation with causality are:

- *Cum hoc ergo propter hoc, Latin for "with this, therefore because of this,"* and

- *Post hoc ergo propter hoc, Latin for "after this, therefore because of this."*

A famous example to illustrate the first fallacy is the fact that Mark Twain was born in 1835 and died in 1910. Both events occurred within days of Halley's Comet passing over Earth. In 1909 Mark Twain wrote: "I came in with Halley's comet in 1835. It is coming again next year, and I expect to go out with it. It will be the greatest disappointment of my life if I don't go out with Halley's Comet. The Almighty has said, no doubt: 'Now here are these two unaccountable freaks; they came in together, they must go out together.'" Obviously, the passing of the comet did not cause the writer's birth or death, even though it may seem that way to the untrained eye.

The second fallacy is probably the most common basis of superstitions. Black cats crossing your path, broken mirrors, and observing three sixes are all considered superstitious signs of bad luck; while knocking on wood, wearing a lucky charm, and crossing your fingers are all superstitions associated with good luck. With enough time between the superstitious act or observation and an event that is interpreted as something that was caused by good luck or bad luck, the causality seems to work.

Going back to the study of the mortgage division and Figure 5.2, the correlations observed based on interviews suggest causation but cannot prove it. The fact that the study was based on interviewing people, who are already loyal, is one way to factor out the dimension of the customer experience that leads to loyalty. In our case that is piece-of-mind. Alternatively, interviewing those who decided not to stay loyal and borrowed at another bank may have revealed that the switch was due to pricing or better customer service, which falls into the other dimensions. If that was the case, that would have revealed that the reasons for switching are not due to not having enough of the reasons for staying, such as piece-of-mind. This may explain why some companies offer better deals for new customers while trying to convince the existing customers to stay when an opportunity arises.

The subject of correlation and causation has been around for centuries. Correlation is more mathematical or statistical in nature. The outcome of the measurement of correlation is probability or predictability between two things, values, or subjects. Causality is more physical or philosophical in nature. In Aristotelian philosophy, a cause would be discovered as the result of looking for answers to "why" questions. The scientific explanation of causality relies on experiments that adhere to strict rules. If you recall how we looked at job dissatisfaction and satisfaction you may recall that we have established that the terms reside on two different planes that do not overlap. While correlations and causality do overlap, it happens far less frequent than we think, and it is, therefore, helpful to keep the two separate.

In everyday life, we are constantly making predictions about outcomes based on our previous experiences. Whether our predictions come true or not, the process gives us a sense of certainty. Even if we think something bad is about to happen, it gives us more comfort than the uncertainty. The effect of uncertainty on one's emotional health has been compared to the effect of an allergic reaction because an allergy can wreak havoc on one's health. At the turn of the 21st Century, a new term was coined.

Intolerance of Uncertainty.

It is a vicious cycle. In an effort to create comfort through attaining certainty, we seek reassurance from others and avoid potentially uncomfortable situations. Unable to get 100% of reassurance or to avoid all the undesirable situations, we may try harder next time, thus the cycle continues. While the topic of intolerance of uncertainty is fairly interesting by itself, the methodology of creating a tool that would measure where a person in a group ends up on an intolerance of uncertainty scale (IUS) is just as fascinating. Once again, there is a creation of a measurement tool that is specific to an objective or goal. The Goal, in this case, is to help with the diagnosis of anxiety disorders that a person with a high IUS score may have. Below is a 27 item questionnaire that was originally developed in 1994 by a team of Quebec psychologists.[2] The participants are asked to rank themselves on a 1-5 scale, 1 being "Not at all characteristic of me," 3 being "Somewhat characteristic of me," and 5 being "Entirely characteristic of me."

1. Uncertainty stops me from having a firm opinion.

2. Being uncertain means that a person is disorganized.

3. Uncertainty makes life intolerable.

4. It's unfair not having any guarantees in life.

5. My mind can't be relaxed if I don't know what will happen tomorrow.

6. Uncertainty makes me uneasy, anxious, or stressed.

7. Unforeseen events upset me greatly.

8. It frustrates me not having all the information I need.

9. Uncertainty keeps me from living a full life.

10. One should always look ahead so as to avoid surprises.

11. A small unforeseen event can spoil everything, even with the best of planning.

12. When it is time to act, uncertainty paralyses me.

13. Being uncertain means that I am not first rate.

14. When I am uncertain I cannot go forward.

15. When I am uncertain I can't function very well.

16. Unlike me, others always seem to know where they are going with their lives.

17. Uncertainty makes me vulnerable, unhappy, or sad.

18. I always want to know what the future has in store for me.

19. I cannot stand being taken by surprise.

20. The smallest doubt can stop me from acting.

21. I should be able to organize everything in advance.

22. Being uncertain means that I lack confidence.

23. I think it's unfair that other people seem so sure about their future.

24. Uncertainty keeps me from sleeping soundly.

25. I must get away from all uncertain situations.

26. The ambiguities in life stress me.

27. I cannot stand being undecided about my future.

Have you recognized yourself reading these statements? I certainly have! The important distinction to be made is between normal and excessive worrying. The first kind is a worry about a high probability of a negative outcome, like experiencing discomfort or worry before getting into a dental chair. The second kind is a constant worrying about what might happen the next day or next week. Constant worrying might be a sign of a serious condition that only a professional can assess. A technique called Worry Tree, depicted in Figure 5.3, may prove useful to reduce the amount of normal worrying.[3]

Fig. 5.3

THE WORRY TREE

1. NOTICE THE WORRY.

2. ASK: WHAT AM I
WORRYING ABOUT?

3. ASK: CAN I DO
SOMETHING ABOUT IT?

NO.   YES.

LET WORRY GO.   ACTION PLAN.

CHANGE FOCUS   WHAT? WHEN? HOW?
OF ATTENTION.

NOW.   LATER

DO IT!   SCHEDULE IT.

LET WORRY GO.   LET WORRY GO.

CHANGE FOCUS   CHANGE FOCUS
OF ATTENTION.   OF ATTENTION.

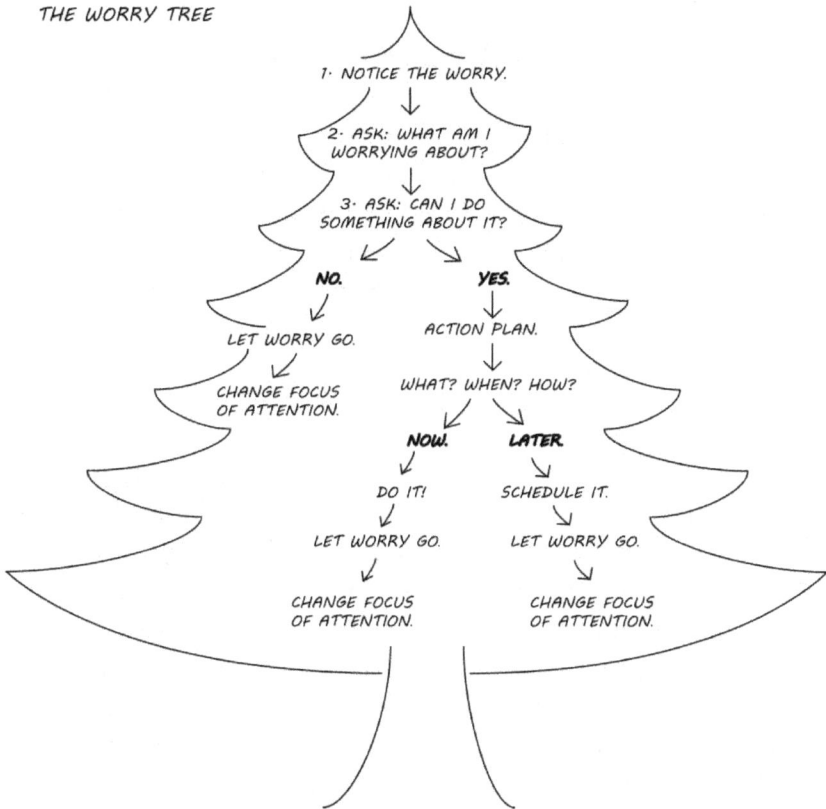

Let's review what we have covered in the chapter thus far. Life Goals can be somewhat ambiguous with a less than clear desirable outcome that would indicate that we are approaching the Goal. Thus, the first step is to gain clarity of our Goals and the desirable outcomes that would indicate that the Goal is near. The next step is to design a Measurement Wheel that will analyze Actions on a periodic basis. The best Measurement tools are custom-built to our Goals and Actions. Just like in the case of measuring a non-physical matter like that of a customer experience, or intolerance of uncertainty, we should employ as many resources as needed and stay clear of any fallacies of logic or reasoning.

The Wheel of Measurements and the Wheel of Goals are in alignment when they are in equal partnership with each other. The ability to accurately measure things is important; however, it is no substitute for a goal that is clearly defined first. For example, if a goal is to find more meaning in life, then the first step is to define what finding meaning in life is. This task may be a bit daunting. At the same time, if by "meaning in life" we mean something else, a purpose, for instance, then defining it may be easier. We really have to spend time honing our thoughts about what it is that we are trying to achieve, for some of the thoughts may be diamonds in the rough.

Goals vs. Process.

As I have mentioned in previous chapters, society plays an important role in the formation of Beliefs and Values. A goal-oriented Western society implemented goal setting to motivate line employees and its management in a post-industrial society. Over time, personal goal setting became the new norm. In my recent research, I've come across some publications that suggest that up to 80% of people do not proactively set goals. Being skeptical, I would accept that 50% of people don't set personal goals. While it may seem high, setting personal goals is not the only way to reach personal success. For centuries, the pursuit of personal excellence was associated with a process of improving one's traits, character, or craft. Nowadays, personal development combines parts of Western and Eastern cultures and includes the following areas of development:

- self-awareness

- self-knowledge

- skills

- self-esteem

- talent and strengths

- wealth

- potential

- Human Capital

- lifestyle

- health

- aspirations

- personal autonomy

- social abilities

Some recommend focusing on processes rather than Goals. For example, if the goal is to run a marathon, one should focus on a training schedule. As a personal example, walking on a treadmill has been the best exercise to keep my weight within a healthy range. As the weight gets outside that range, I concentrate on finding time to walk 2-3 miles a day until I log 62.5 miles or 100 kilometers. I call it a 100K challenge. While the goal is to lose weight, I concentrate on walking every day until I reach the 100K mark. This makes my goal a byproduct of the process. Is that just a mind trick to take a break from the burnout of having too many Goals, or Goals that are too big? Yes. Goals for the sake of Goals can be counterproductive. A great example of this is a working paper, *Goals Gone Wild*.[4]

Below are some pitfalls that were identified in that paper. I have purposefully omitted specific examples to let you think of examples of your own. They can be something that you have experienced or something that you can see happening.

1. **When Goals Are Too Specific** – As research has shown, goals focus attention. Unfortunately, goals can

focus attention so narrowly that people overlook other important features of a task.

2. **Narrow Goals** – With goals, people narrow their focus. This focus can blind people to important issues that appear unrelated to their goals.

3. **Too Many Goals** – A related problem occurs when employees pursue multiple goals at one time. Related research suggests that some types of goals are more likely to be ignored than others. When quantity and quality goals were both difficult, participants sacrificed the quality to meet the quantity goals because quantity was easier to measure.

4. **Inappropriate Time Horizon** – Even if goals are set on the right attribute, the time horizon may be inappropriate. For example, goals that emphasize immediate performance (e.g., this quarter's profits) prompt managers to engage in myopic, short-term behaviors that may harm the organization in the long run.

5. **When Goals Are Too Challenging** – Proponents of goal setting claim that a positive linear relationship exists between the difficulty of a goal and employee performance. This logic makes intuitive sense, yet stretch goals also cause serious side-effects: shifting risk attitudes, promoting unethical behavior, and triggering the psychological costs of goal failure.

6. **Risk Taking** – Goal setting distorts risk preferences. People motivated by specific challenging goals adopt riskier strategies and choose riskier gambles than do those with less challenging or vague goals.

7. **Unethical Behavior** – Goal setting can promote two different types of cheating behavior. First, when motivated by a goal, people may choose to use unethical methods to reach it. Second, goal setting can motivate people to misrepresent their performance level – in other words, to report that they met a goal when in fact they fell short.

8. **Dissatisfaction and the Psychological Consequences of Goal Failure** – One problem in stretch goals is the possibility that the goal may not be reached. Challenging goals can increase task performance, but decrease satisfaction with high-quality outcomes. These decreases in satisfaction influence how people view themselves and have important consequences for future behavior. These goal-induced reductions in self-efficacy can be highly detrimental, because perceptions of self-efficacy are a key predictor of task engagement, commitment, and effort.

9. **Goals Inhibit Learning** – When individuals face a complex task, specific, challenging goals may inhibit learning from experience and degrade performance compared to exhortations to "do your best." An individual who is narrowly focused on a performance goal will be less likely to try alternative methods that could help her learn how to perform a task.

10. **Goals Create a Culture of Competition** – Organizations that rely heavily on goal setting may erode the foundation of cooperation that holds groups together. Exclusive focus on profit maximization can harm altruistic and other regarding behavioral motives. Similarly, being too focused on achieving a specific goal may decrease extra-role behavior, such as helping coworkers. Goals may promote competition rather than cooperation and ultimately lower overall performance.

11. **When Goals Harm Motivation Itself** – As goal setting increases extrinsic motivation, it can harm intrinsic motivation – engaging in a task for its own sake. Managers may think that others need to be motivated by specific, challenging goals far more often than they actually do.

12. **Can We Set the Right Goal? The Problem of Calibration** – Proponents of goal setting have long championed the simplicity of its implementation and the efficiency of its effects. In practice, however, setting goals is a challenging process, especially in novel settings. Goal setting can become problematic when the same goal is applied to many different people. Conversely, idiosyncratically tailoring goals to each individual can lead to charges of unfairness. This has important implications, because employee perceptions of whether rewards fairly match effort and performance can be one of the best predictors of commitment and motivation.

Exercise.

Think about the twelve problems identified above. On a piece of paper write down what Wheel of the Model each problem will effect and why. Refer to Chapter One as needed.

Outcomes vs. Outputs.

The Measurements Wheel can be set up to measure outcomes or output of the Wheel of Actions. In the case of the mortgage division of a major UK bank, we looked at the desired outcomes. Are outcomes that much different from outputs, or just semantics? Yes, there is a deeper difference. The following will help you to remember it.

Think about the production of automobiles. The number of units produced per year is an annual output. Some car manufacturers produce more cars and trucks than others. They have different outputs. When you think about which car or truck you like and why, do you think about the output? When you think about purchasing your next car or truck what goes into your decision making process? How is that related to output?

Let's take reliability for instance. Are the most reliable cars and trucks also the most produced? If reliability is the desired outcome, how can a manufacturer go about it? Imagine if the next million cars and trucks produced by a major automaker in 2018 had zero defects, no recalls, and even with marginal service, all the vehicles ran for 10 years or 300,000 miles with no need for major part replacement and no signs of rust! Is it possible? If it is, what would these cars and trucks have to cost? Would you be more inclined to buy them at a higher price?

Outcomes are the results of outputs, and as such outcomes can be intended or unintended. In a world of financial profits, the cost of quality may be justified only to a certain level. Making things that last for a very long time could cost so much that hardly anyone will buy them at a profit. Therefore, the products that are mass produced, like consumer electronics, have the intended level of quality that is in line with the price and the expected life of the product. The unintended outcome of mass production could be the case where a pressure from a larger consumer group results in quality improvement. The pressure can take a range of forms, from informal complaints to class action law suits.

In the world of not-for-profit organizations, private contributors, and grant providers, return on investment (ROI) is the focus. The way non-for-profits measure the ROI is to look at the economic impact of the outcomes. Accomplishments and results are the examples of an outcome, while services and activities are the examples of outputs. For instance, charter schools in Michigan are mostly not-for-profit organizations.

They are often tax payer funded and privately managed. The charter schools are part of the K-12 education and the performance of charter school students are measured similarly as public school students. Both have to take statewide tests. In some states, the results of the test, or outcomes, taken by students of charter schools are higher compared to test results of public school students. In other states, the outcomes are the opposite.

In Michigan, charter schools provide educational opportunities in economically challenged areas of Detroit. If a greater Goal is to provide education to as much of the population as possible in an effort to fight illiteracy, then the quality of teaching, or the output, could be compromised due to two main factors. First, the budget of a charter school does not often allow it to employ the teaching talent that is comparable to public schools. Often, the teachers in Detroit charter schools are semi-retired or part time professionals. With a wage disparity factor of 1.5 times or more, it is hard to maintain the level of commitment necessary to engage the inner city students. The second factor is the students. Some students lack the means to get to school and some older students have to work part-time to help their parents. The environment that surrounds the students outside the school can be less than conducive to learning and more conducive to be involved in criminal activities.

As a banker, I worked with several charter schools in Detroit. They were part of church campuses. It was quite an experience to see the joy of learning and to feel the sense of appreciation the students had just from being surrounded by adults who cared about them. These are positive unintended outcomes that charter schools provide in the areas where public schools are simply non-existent.

Chapter Summary.

The original SMART criteria has M for Measurable. We take M completely out and create a dedicated category, the Measurement Wheel. SMART criteria, Version 2.0, as I jokingly call my own interpretation of SMART, offers some degree of Measurement of the progress towards one's Goal. By questioning ourselves and spending some quiet time understanding our own what, why, and how as they relate to our Goals, we will more than compensate for not having a M for Measurable.

The Wheel of Measurement can be looked at as a toolbox. I have an old Craftsman five drawer chest full of poorly organized wrenches, sockets, measuring tapes, levels, and drill bits. I use them once every three to four months and they do the job just fine. The pictures I hang are level. The heavier fixtures are secured by the screws that I masterfully drive into the studs. Finding the center of the stud and verifying the stud finder with a ruler is a process I truly enjoy. However, when we are looking to measure something intangible, a level of loyalty, for instance, we often rely on surveys and interviews. Though not as precise of a measurement compared to a ruler, if taken periodically and in enough quantity, they give us valuable information.

As we have seen in the case with a major UK bank's mortgage division, Goals can be broken down to a level of desired outcomes of Actions. In measuring the outcomes, the tool employed is a sophisticated matrix that reveals a correlation between various factors of the outcomes. The topic of correlation has led us to look at a common fallacy of confusing correlation with causation. This topic is an important one as we make inferences based on our own analysis. This analysis often includes conclusions based on correlations.

When thinking about future outcomes, we are longing for a sense of certainty. It is comforting to think that a plane will leave on time, children will not get into trouble, and our efforts will be rewarded. For some of us, the desire for certainty comes from the inability to cope with uncertainty. A group of Canadian scientists coined the phrase "Intolerance of Uncertainty" to measure the level of how uncomfortable one can be with uncertainty. We also looked at what can be done to reduce the level of uncertainty.

Having too many or too high of Goals can be counterproductive. It can lead to burnout, disappointments, and even unethical behavior. As an alternative, a process focused on Actions can help us achieve goals. This approach works best when the goals do not have tight deadlines.

Concluding the chapter is clarification between outcomes and outputs. The Goals and Measurements can be set for either one; however, a little more clarity now will make one avoid a lot of confusion later. Outcomes could be thought of as high level Goals, while the outputs could be thought of as processes. The key to finding balance is to allow for some flexibility. The best way to align the two Wheels is to customize the Measurements and to be flexible with your Goals.

Chapter Six: Relationship Between Wheels of Goals and Actions.

The discussion that took place up until this point covered the explanation of the Model, left-to-right alignment, and front-to-back alignment of the Wheels. For the next two chapters we will look at the relationships between the wheels in the opposite corners. Even though they do not get aligned relative to each other on real cars, they do in our Model.

So far we looked at SMART criteria for organizational goal setting and the modified SMART criteria for setting personal goals, otherwise known as SMART V 2.0. For those of you who like acronyms, here are two more goal-setting criteria: PURE and CLEAR. Figure 6.1 below summarizes all four.[*]

Fig. 6.1

Original SMART	SMART V 2.0[*]	PURE	CLEAR
Specific	Stretched	Positively Stated	Challenging
Measurable	Memorable	Understood	Legal
Assignable	Aligned	Relevant	Environmentally Sound
Realistic	Resourced	Ethical	Appropriate
Time-Bound	Taskable		Recorded

The positively stated element of PURE is an interesting one. Indeed, the way we state a goal has an immediate impact on how we feel about it. Whether we state a goal out loud or write it down, a positively stated goal will have subtleties that will energize us. For instance, a statement like "my goal is to lose ten pounds" has the negatively charged word "loss" in it. Stated another way, "my goal is to keep a healthy weight" contains the positively charged words "keep" and "healthy."

---

[*] *SMART V 2.0 is my own use of the acronym for setting personal goals.*

For most people these words would have positive connotations. "Challenging" in the CLEAR model sounds very similar to "Stretched." "Recorded" in CLEAR echoes with "Memorable" in SMART V 2.0. There might be some other overlaps of goal setting approaches.

Whether our goals are SMART, PURE, or CLEAR, they may fall into some broader categories of goals. One particular theory illustrates the point. It also fits perfectly between the Wheels of Goals and Actions as it focuses primarily on Goals and Action.

Goal Orientation Theory. (GOT)

Originated from the 1940s works of David McClelland and his colleagues on Achievement Orientation, the theory became important when studying academic motivation in the late 1980s. More recently, the GOT was found valuable when applied to the fields of sports, health, and communications.

According to the theory, goals are divided into two categories. The first category is mastery goals. Mastery goals, also known as mastery orientation, are identified as a desire to increase competence through learning and a way to stay resilient in the face of challenge or failure. Self-improvement is the main theme of this category. The second category is performance goals. Also known as performance orientation, the category deals with an individual's desire to showcase their ability to outperform their peers. Competition is the main theme of this category.

Under the GOT, mastery and performance goals are further broken down into two groups of people. The first group would proactively approach either mastery or performance goals. Therefore, the group is called approach-oriented. The second group would seek to avoid a situation that could jeopardize their status while in pursuit of mastery or performance goals. This group is called avoidance-oriented. Figure 6.2 is a matrix that summarizes the theory.

Fig. 6.2

	Mastery goals	Performance goals
Approach - oriented	Motivated by continuing self-improvement to achieve mastery in competencies	Motivated by competition to perform better then others
Avoidance - oriented	Motivated situations where task is unclear	Motivated situations where may appear incompetent

Avoidance may manifest itself as indecisiveness or delay in action. These manifestations may be seen as a weakness and are often the topic of discussion during life coaching sessions. While keeping a client in a judgement-free space, the coaching process is designed to move a client towards his or her goals which may or may not include reducing the avoidance.

Think about where you may be falling within the above matrix. (Figure 6.2) The reality is that you may have multiple goals and orientations in your life. You may be striving for mastery in photography and proudly displaying pictures of people and nature. Meanwhile, you may be using lack of time as an excuse to avoid public speaking opportunities to share your expertise.

Life's journey is similar to a road trip in terms of moving towards a certain destination while trying to avoid getting lost, hitting other vehicles on the road, and running out of gas. That's why our cars have one pedal for "go," one pedal for "stop," and a steering system to maintain or change our direction. A car that cannot get out of the way, break or control its direction is unsafe.

There is something to be said about night driving. The headlights make just a few hundred feet visible, yet we can drive at night for hours and travel hundreds of miles. Why are we comfortable going beyond the visible? The answer is simple. We have an unwavering faith that the road is not going to end beyond what we can see, or we will have time to react if it does. The longer we drive, the more comfortable we get. Why does that same principle not apply to other areas of our lives? Why are we reluctant to try something new, unless we are guaranteed the desired outcomes? We use phrases like "I don't see myself doing this" or "I can't see myself being like so-and-so."

No meaningful Goals have been reached without Actions. Also, as you may recall from Chapter One, Figure 1.5, Actions can be either visible or invisible. Thinking is an example of an invisible Action. Thinking is just as important as a visible Action when we are working towards our Goals. The way we think plays a crucial role in our lives and, therefore, warrants a closer examination.

The way we think.

Our Actions, including thinking, are mostly habitual. Habits make us more efficient—regardless of whether the habits we develop are healthy or unhealthy—as habitual Actions require less energy. You may wonder what some of the healthy or unhealthy thinking habits may be. Let me share a few examples.

Healthy thinking habits.

Start your day with a mindset of abundance. A new day is full of opportunities, and what may have happened yesterday is in the past. Doing morning exercises, eating a healthy breakfast, and listening to upbeat music on the way to work should help to set a joyful mood.

A watercooler conversation about bad weather or traffic will undoubtedly engage many participants. We love complaining, yet the outcome of such conversation is neutral at best. Sharing positive comments about a movie you have recently watched or a book you have recently read is a better alternative as it will send out a positive vibe. The small change of thinking before talking may require a lot of conscious effort, but it is worth it. Give it a shot!

The name of my coaching practice is Positive Coaching. Positive, as opposed to negative, is the desired direction on the negative / positive continuum and also the desired state of mind. The goal is not to avoid challenges, conflicts, and other unpleasant realities in life, but to look for and recognize the moments to cherish. A positive mindset starts with an effort to describe people and things around you using positive language.

You will be surprised how much your overall well-being will improve once you adopt a positive way of thinking.

The way we think about problems is often one area where we can all improve. Generalizing and catastrophizing does not require much effort; yet they do not provide any real solutions. Learning from previous mistakes is the way to keep moving forward. Combining self-trust with positive thinking may sound obvious, but how often do you practice it during your everyday interactions?

Healthy thinking habits also include gratitude. There are several ways to practice gratitude from the simple acts of smiling and enjoying the outdoors to keeping a daily journal and sending Thank You cards to friends, family, and colleagues. The idea is to focus on and be grateful for people and things that we already have in our lives. Happiness does not have to be tied to some future event. Here and now is just as perfect if we allow it to be.

The "be careful what you wish for, you just might get it" expression comes from observing the correlation between wishful thinking and the wish materialization. Some may even argue causality. In 1911, Franklin Roosevelt said "there is nothing I love as much as a good fight." Thirty-three years later, as the Commander-in-Chief, he got a chance to lead the US troops as they landed in Normandy to join the Allies against the Nazi Germany army, thereby entering the biggest fight of the 20th Century. We cannot always control the outcome of the many events that make up our lives, but we can control our attitude. This control comes from the way we think.

Developing healthy thinking habits, just like any other habits, will require time, conscious effort, and support. That said, the change is worth the effort. Some studies have suggested a strong connection between a healthy mind and a healthy body. Other studies claim that positive thinking is a key to longevity. Whatever your reasons may be to allow for more cheer and joy in your life, positivity in your thinking is the key. If you are not already inspired by the paragraphs you just read, you may be influenced by reading the paragraphs that follow.

Unhealthy thinking habits.

If your life is filled largely with self-doubt and low levels of self-trust and self-confidence, unhealthy thinking habits may be the culprit. You may think you have a reason to think negatively about your life. For instance, you may be having a hard time getting ahead in your occupation or your personal life is not what you think it should be. Discouraged, you may engage in thinking that your current state of affairs is due to some factors that are outside of your control. You may think that some people or organizations are out to get you. You may even start to think that you were born to live an unhappy life.

Science is providing more and more evidence that hereditary predispositions do not account for one's fortune or misfortune as much as scientists used to believe in the past. Even if we have been dealt a deck of less-than-perfect genes, we still have a chance at living a good life if we don't dwell on negative thoughts more than necessary. Figure 5.3 in Chapter 5 provides a good framework for thinking about a difficult situation. Answering the question "can I do something about the situation?" is an opportunity to change the situation or maintain your current position. Change often requires a new way of thinking. That new way of thinking then needs to be followed by visible Action.

You may wonder where negative thinking comes from in the first place. The answer has two parts.

First, we are hard-wired not to take Action during much of our childhood because of a perceived danger. We were taught not to talk to strangers and not to walk in a neighborhood without adult supervision. To show respect, we were taught not to argue with the elderly. It is easy to see how these and other prohibitions, if taken into adulthood and combined with other negative experiences, could result in a negative bias. Those of us who dared to talk, walk, and argue when we were not supposed to may have been disciplined or punished. Therefore, when Action is required, we may talk ourselves out of taking it by thinking that it will be of no use or the outcome will be negative.

Second, as adults, we often associate being realistic with outcomes that are less than we originally hoped for. This way, we would not get disappointed in ourselves or others. What do we usually mean when we say "get real?" Don't we usually imply that one's expectations are higher than our own? How many times do we tell ourselves to "get real?" Depending on how strong our negative bias is, it may influence our perception of reality and stop us from taking Actions.

If you are having hard to control negative thoughts that are getting in the way of your daily activities, or if you find yourself being mostly sad, upset or withdrawn, please consult a medical professional.

Overcoming negative thinking.

Negative thoughts are a part of life. They are also part of a normal psyche. You might be a successful professional, happy at home, and may not feel that negative thoughts are negatively affecting your life. In that case, I would not advocate changing the way you think unless you feel the need to reduce the number of negative thoughts or you want to increase the number of positive ones. If increasing the number of positive thoughts you have is a goal, these tips might help.

1. Smile right this instant! Notice the immediate change in thoughts coming in. We tend to smile as a reaction to

positive thoughts or feelings, therefore, smiling helps to connect with positive thoughts and emotions. To take this exercise to the next level, try laughing for no reason. Warning: once you start, it may be hard to stop!

2. Don't get down on yourself for having negative thoughts. Instead, look for ways to change your attention to something positive. Focus on a view outside the window, or on upbeat music being played on the radio, or think of a memory of a recent experience that made you happy. Try to keep your attention focused on that happy thought for at least a few minutes.

3. Analyze the situations, places, and people that you are surrounded by. Where do your most positive vibes come from? Is the source of positivity good for your body and your mind? Remember that not all that makes us happy is good for us. Avoid quick fixes that you know are harmful in the long run. They may contribute to negative thinking later, as they may show up as regrets or illnesses, or both.

4. Are you watching your diet? Foods that are rich in calcium, magnesium, iron, and omega-3 have been cited to promote physical and emotional well-being. Personally, I can get away with a moderate amount of pick-me-up carbs, sugars, fats, and caffeine.

5. Physical activity and exercise are just as important as a healthy diet. Once again, moderation is the key. Come up with a routine that you can commit to. Switch it up several times a year. Let yourself gain some weight if your priorities have shifted to something more important than time in the gym. Come back when physical fitness is a priority again. The mistake we often make is when we are not allowing any flexibility in our schedules. The older we get, the more likely we are to have competing

priorities associated with growing children, aging parents, and the increasing responsibilities at work. Keep that smile on as you juggle the balls!

Exercise.

Below are some questions that will help you focus on positive thinking by reminding yourself how children experience happiness and joy in their lives.

1. Recall a happy memory of your childhood. What made you happy?

2. Look at your nephew, nieces, cousins, children, or grandchildren that are seven years of age or younger. What makes them happy? Is it a certain activity, a particular toy, or a person in their life? What about that particular activity, toy, or person makes them happy?

3. Observe the interaction between children on a playground. Observe the interaction between the children and their parents or grandparents. Which interaction brings more happiness to the children? Why?

Science behind positive thinking and optimism.

Unfortunately, positivity and optimism often get a bad rap. In my research, I have come across numerous articles where the writers share their stories of being ridiculed when letting their naturally happy personality shine. I have also observed it in person. One of the reasons for this is that there are fake optimists that we have all most likely dealt with in the past. The person may have been over the top and led us to feel inadequate in some way. The second reason I see is the lack of trust in anything that resembles a person or idea that we may have believed in, or even spent time and money following, and realized that we were sold a bill of goods. While these experiences are painful at times, they should not force us into gloom.

A fascinating study conducted over 30 years ago by Michael Scheier and Charles Carver looked at benefits of positive thinking and optimism in several areas of life.[1] Since its original publication in 1985, the work has been referenced in over 3,000 publications and it is certainly worth to include in our discussion. Below are some important observations that stood the test of time and gained additional support from the experts.

1. Some people are inherently more optimistic than others. It is unclear as to why; however, the main trait of an optimistic person is the expectation of a positive outcome of their actions.

2. Inability to understand the root cause of optimism led the authors to assume that it is either prior experience in reaching goals that softens the blow of challenges that the person encounters, or it is the fact that more optimistic people address challenges as soon as they are aware of them. In the latter case, it is easier to deal with problems that have not been ignored and, therefore, new problems will likely be solved. As the result of the positive and proactive approaches, optimists reported less stress in their lives.

I solved problems before,
I can solve this problem too!

I have a problem.
I better handle it as soon as possible!

3. Women that scored high on optimism seem to be less affected by post-partum depression. The reason for that was positive thinking. It was the main factor that allowed coping with depression. A proactive approach to problem solving was also helpful in coping with post-partum depression.

4. The study discovered an inverse correlation between optimism and emotional expression and with disengagement from the goal. This suggested that in the presence of an adverse event, optimists did not dwell on negative emotions and remained engaged in goal-reaching activities. On the other hand, pessimism and negative thinking was correlated with emotional fixation on the problem and lack of action.

5. Physiological benefits of optimism, in the words of Michael Scheier during his 2012 interview: "A smaller, but still substantial, amount of research has studied associations [of optimism] with physical well-being. And I think most researchers at this point would agree that optimism is connected to positive physical health outcomes, including decreases in the likelihood of re-hospitalization following surgery, the risk of developing heart disease, and mortality." [2]

Less focus on negative emotions and more focus on Actions towards attaining Goals is a way positive thinking shows up and defines true optimism. While it seems like a good idea to adopt an optimistic perspective, many prefer to stay realistic, or even openly admit and defend a pessimistic viewpoint on life. For years, I have been asking the question of why I see so much negatively charged thinking, full of low expectation of self and others. One day my question was answered in a profound way.

A useful reference.

I have had the privilege to chair a very special group called the Leadership Enrichment Council. This group is a part of the Troy Chamber of Commerce and consists of its members. The number of monthly attendees varies from 15 to 25 and includes professionals and small business owners. For two years I was responsible for finding guest speakers and book reviewers. During our time together, the group reviewed dozens of books, but one particular book stood out. That book was *Power vs. Force* by David R. Hawkins.

I remember how the presentation captivated all the participants and kept them on the edge of their seats until the very end. It took two meetings to go over the 17 levels, and I will never forget the group's reaction as members recited the text that explained each level in detail. The body language and facial expressions demonstrated a strong connection with the book. I often think about it as a great concept and a useful reference. As such, it has its place in this part of our discussion of thinking, for the level of consciousness that we are in during any given moment has a direct effect on our thoughts.

Figure 6.3 on the following page shows various levels of being. I use this word in a broader sense to include physical, emotional, and spiritual components.[3]

Fig. 6.3

MAP OF CONCIOUSNESS

Life-View *	Level	Log**	Emotion
Is	Enlightenment	700-1,000	Ineffable
Perfect	Peace	600	Bliss
Complete	Joy	540	Serenity
Benign	Love	500	Reverence
Meaningful	Reason	400	Understanding
Harmonious	Acceptance	350	Forgiveness
Hopeful	Willingness	310	Optimism
Satisfactory	Neutrality	250	Trust
Feasible	Courage	200	Affirmation
Demanding	Pride	175	Scorn
Antagonistic	Anger	150	Hate
Disappointing	Desire	125	Craving
Frightening	Fear	100	Anxiety
Tragic	Grief	75	Regret
Hopeless	Apathy	50	Despair
Evil	Guilt	30	Blame
Miserable	Shame	20	Humiliation

* Perspective or the outlook on life.
** As measured by a system created by Dr. Hawkins.

According to David Hawkins, levels from shame to pride, Log 20 – 175, represent destructive powers, while levels from courage to enlightenment are constructive powers. An individual's level is a sum of levels in different areas of the person's life. For instance, one can be a courageous stunt performer that can jump from tall buildings and walk into a room full of poisonous snakes. Meanwhile, he or she will get angry at times when watching the news.

The practical application of the Map of Consciousness is in awareness of the following. It does not take much effort, or energy, to create and maintain destructive states and negative emotions. It hardy takes any effort to shame, blame, judge, fear, yell, and hate. The mental ease of dwelling on negativity is the reason it's so popular and omnipresent. On the other side, levels above 650 are only achieved by individuals who can afford a life outside of every day events and spend most of their time praying or meditating. Therefore, this level is not applicable for most of us. It is included in the map to complete the scale. The levels from 250 to 500 will require a great deal of effort to attain, but they offer worthwhile experiences.

Exercise.

Think about your current overall level as depicted in Figure 6.3. What situations in your life influence upward or downward movement? What can be done to attain and sustain a desired level?

Law of Attraction.

I get involved in conversations regarding practical applications of the Law of Attraction (LOA) at least once a month, sometimes weekly. I remember my own fascination when I saw *The Secret* and then I read the book by the same title, and I can say that the maxim "like attracts like" attracted me. The book found me at a fork in the road of a personal journey. I was confused and lacking trust toward anyone, including myself, and decided to give LOA a try. It worked.

Almost a decade later, reflecting back to the time of my commitment to LOA, I can see why it worked. First, it forced me to get clear on the things I wanted in my life, and at the same time realize the things I was running away from. It was hard and required focus. In the process I began visualizing my ideal future which, by the virtue of my own way of thinking, provided reasoning and answered why I wanted what I wanted. Still, nothing new was really happening in my life until I started to execute on my plan towards the ideal future.

For the next year, I had taken an amount of Action I never thought I could take. Deep inside I knew that this was a time of transformation and put my all into attainment of the ideal future. The law of attraction, in practical terms, is a law of attainment. I could not have become the person I am today, and have the people in my life I have today, without engaging in massive Action.

Thinking vs Doing.

Thinking is a powerful Action that accomplishes very little in the physical world. For any thoughts to materialize into a tangible substance there has to be a visible Action. Doing is required for any of your dreams to come true. As thought-provoking as this book may be, it has very little value if your thoughts are not followed by Actions. Talking, writing, building, selling, advising, caring, exercising, eating, resting, reading, feeding, fighting, hiding, doing dishes, listening, playing, sleeping, and many other activities are required not to just get ahead in life, but to maintain the life we already have. Doing also requires us to destroy parts of life that are no longer of value.

Metaphorically speaking, things happen to us just as much as we happen to them. We get up and we walk until we get on a certain path of life. On that path we meet other people from whom we learn and who we teach. They become part of our successes and failures just as much as we become theirs.

I get upset when psychologists are against black-and-white thinking, yet it is perfectly fine for some of them to verse thinking mindset and doing mindset. This simple comparison is black-and-white thinking. Our minds are more complex than that. However, we need to be doing things to survive, maintain life, and to get ahead. So why we don't do what we know we are supposed to be doing? Here are some explanations.

1. Laziness. As I am writing this, I've realized that I have not posted new videos to my YouTube channel for

about a month. I love making videos outside, but today is a cold winter day. It is also windy. I can go on and on with reasons for not making a video, yet the voice of my conscience tells me: "Be honest, you just don't want to put the effort in; just admit to being lazy." I did. Realizing that at the moment I am not practicing what I am preaching, I stopped writing, went outside, and made the video. After I came back I was proud of my abilities of overcoming myself. Let me assure you that I do not act the way I should every time I admit to laziness. Sometimes, I just remain inactive, rationalizing that the inaction preserves energy for when it is really needed. Does this sound familiar? Can you relate?

2. Fear. As I wrote the paragraph above, the same voice that guilt-tripped me into getting outside was questioning if I might offend my reader by suggesting that they are lazy. It was also questioning whether or not my reader might perceive me as weak if I admit to being lazy. Had I continued on this path, and implemented this line of thinking to other parts of the book, I would have risked convincing myself to abandon the manuscript for the fear that the book might not be well-received. Therefore, if you are reading this passage, I have found a way to overcome my own fear. Also, I hope I did not offend you.

3. HALT. This abbreviation stands for hungry, angry, lonely, and tired. Are you experiencing any of these conditions at the moment? If so, you might not be in the best position to make important decisions and act on them. That being said, is it possible not to be HALT? Is there a reliable system that would monitor our level of HALT so that we can make better decisions and have our actions bring more success and happiness to our lives? The answer is no. We have to come up with our own system through trial and error. Making sure that we

get good quality sleep and regular meals is the foundation that also helps with emotional and social aspects of being angry or lonely. The awareness of our emotional and physical well-being is the first step towards planning our Actions. Should you take care of yourself before you take care of business? Only you can answer.

4. Choices. The beauty of leading your own life is the fact that you get to decide what action to take first. You get to call your own shots. Is the freedom to choose the ultimate attraction that can fuel a massive action? Not always. With freedom of choice comes responsibility for the decisions we make and the actions we take. Sometimes, we just refuse to step up to the plate. For each of us the reason is different. It may be laziness, fear, HALT, lack of support, lack of information, or any combination thereof. Nevertheless, as long as we know, understand, and accept the fact that growth comes from taking on more responsibilities, we will eventually rise to the occasion and take the first step.

5. Past Experience. We owe our past for all the successes we celebrate today, yet we tend to remember negative experiences more than positive and, sometimes, we even let negative experiences hold us back. The older we get the more negative experiences we accumulate. At the same time, some studies have shown that some of the happiest people are well into their 70s and 80s. While this may be true, some of us have a few decades to live before reaching our 70s and 80s. As a way to overcome the inertia and gain some momentum, I suggest that we develop routines that we stick with for a period of time. It takes two to three months to develop a habit. What habit do you wish you had? Why?

6. What's the Rush? I suspect this question has stopped a lot of Action for people that answered: "There is no rush." Indeed, why should we speed up going in a certain direction? I really don't like the answer I am about to offer, but we all have 24 hours a day, and we don't know how many days we have left. I know this may sound harsh, but if you need a boost to your sense of urgency, that thought should help. What would be one thing that you would want to achieve by the end of this week or this month?

7. Can't Stop. As hard as developing a new habit may be, it may be even harder to break a habit that is no longer serving you. Therefore, we need to look at our Actions in relative terms and use words like "more" and "less." Time and energy saved by doing less of one thing is a precious gift. What would you do with an extra hour of time if you had it available every day?

Cycles of Actions.

When I was attending my undergraduate studies, many required classes in Economics, English, and Accounting were offered during the 1:00 p.m. – 3:00 p.m. window. I can't tell you how many times I embarrassed myself by falling asleep and waking up from my own snoring. It did not matter who was teaching, where I sat in the classroom, or how big the classroom was. The only thing that mattered was the time of day. Even after graduation, I found it hard to concentrate during that timeframe. Eventually, my sleeping spells were cured with an increased caffeine intake and the fear of losing my first full-time job.

There is a scientific explanation of what was happening to me. Some of you may have heard about circadian rhythm. This is a biological clock observed in animals and humans. It is responsible for physiological processes such as metabolism and blood pressure. The cycle in humans is about 24 hours and it affects our sleep. Some studies suggest that adults experience strongest sleep drives between 2:00 a.m. – 4:00 a.m. and between 1:00 p.m. – 3:00 p.m. Equally important is the exposure to natural lighting. In its absence, the circadian cycle will eventually shift. If you have ever experienced jet leg, you have experienced an effect of a changed circadian cycle. Being aware of our biological clocks, we can experiment with switching up the activities accordingly. For instance, you can align the time period that you are more energetic with the type of activity that requires the most energy. Alternatively, if there is no option for such alignment, be proactive and make necessary adjustments to boost your energy.

Within the 24 hour circadian rhythm, there are several ultradian rhythms that are 90-120 minutes in duration. They are part of sleep stages, hormonal secretion, heart rate, and functions of the digestive system, to name a few. Aligning our biological schedules with our business schedules just makes sense. Everything else being equal, the individuality of biological rhythms affects the efficiency and effectiveness of our Actions.

Energy management.

From time to time we all feel tired and unable to carry on without slowing down or taking a break. However, should your energy level decrease and stay low for days or weeks and affect your day to day activities, you may have a medical condition. In case of a prolonged fatigue, please seek medical attention. Somewhere in between brief and temporary physical and mental exhaustion and a diagnosed condition, lies a gray area that I'd like to address. Below are my thoughts that come from my own experience. I share them for you to consider.

The goal of energy management is to maintain a certain level of your mental and physical energy throughout the day and align it with daily activities. For simplicity, let's consider three levels.

1. Rest. This level is for activities that require minimal physical and mental energy. Examples include watching TV or surfing the net before going to bed.

2. Routine. This level is for activities that require a fair amount of physical energy, but are performed with minimal amount of mental energy. Examples include doing laundry, driving to and from work, and simple tasks performed at work, such as checking email and voicemail.

3. Performance. This level is for activities that require the most mental energy, and may also require a fair amount of physical energy. Examples include driving through a busy downtown for the first time, being interviewed for a job, having a difficult conversation, or solving unexpected problems.

When you are at work, your activities require a frequent change between the routine and performance levels. Ideally, you would start your day with some routine activities to settle in and get ready for more difficult tasks. Unfortunately, this is not what typically happens. How many times have you tried to plan your day the night before and have your first unexpected problem waiting for you as soon as you arrive? By the time you put the fire out, it is time to address the problems on your planner. Will you have physical energy and mental focus to continue to perform? Since we have already touched on the importance of a good night's sleep, and we talked about HALT, I would invite you to consider some popular ways to boost your energy. Keep in mind, individual results may vary.

1. Seek out and communicate with positive people throughout the day. These may be your friends and

family members, coworkers, or even online chat pals. Lifting each other emotionally is a great way to provide your mind a quick rest and re-energize it at the same time.

2. The "breakfast is the most important meal of the day" advice is old and accumulated enough claims that suggest causality between high fiber foods like oatmeal consumed in the morning and less fatigue throughout the day.

3. For a quick energy boost, foods that are high in folic acid and magnesium, like almonds and peanuts, are often recommended. Cinnamon has been reported to have a similar energy-boosting effect. Obviously, people that have nut and cinnamon allergies would have to find an alternative.

4. Staying hydrated has also been linked with higher levels of energy. When you feel tired, a glass of water may do the trick.

5. Running low on blood sugar may also cause a drop in mental and physical energy. For a long-term effect, slow-burning carbs found in rye bread, oatmeal, banana, brown rice and most vegetables have been cited.

6. Spending a little time outside, under the sun, has been known to help improve emotional and mental health. If you can't break away, letting sunlight into your room is a great alternative.

7. Last but not least, physical exercise is a great energy booster because it delivers oxygen-rich blood to all parts of our body. If you don't have time for regular exercise and you have a desk job, consider taking frequent breaks to stand up, stretch, and walk around.

Chapter Summary.

No matter which methodology we utilize to set Goals, the way we think about Goals and what we do to achieve them play an important role. What outcome do we expect and why? How do we go about reaching our Goals? These are the overarching questions of the chapter; thus, the focus is on Actions.

The way we think is a reflection of who we are and a good predictor of our behavior. If we want to change who we are, we need to be aware of our thinking habits. Our thoughts do follow certain patterns. The good news is the existing patterns can be broken and new ones established. Both positive and negative thinking were examined for their respective pros and cons.

As in previous chapters, I've included some scientific backing to my own thoughts. It is easy to engage in thinking based on limited or incorrect information offered online. Also, I often catch myself wanting to believe in something that is just too good to be true. Alternatively, like in the case of my personal experience with LOA, a fresh perspective can break a pattern of thinking that can no longer support personal or professional goals.

The brain, our thinking engine, needs energy to run effectively and efficiently. Thus, I've shared a few thoughts regarding energy and its sources and uses. The uniqueness of our bodies cannot be discounted. What is a good diet or exercise system for one may be detrimental to another. I simply invite you to consider the ideas and try what you think might work based on your own assessment. The important part is not just to consider, but to act on your consideration. Whether you take a giant leap, or a baby step, is entirely up to you.

Chapter Seven: Relationship Between the Wheels of Beliefs and Values and Measurements.

In Chapter Five I have suggested that Measurements are part of Goals. We have also seen how much effort goes into creating methods of measuring and interpreting the results. In this chapter I am going to suggest that Measurements are also part of Beliefs and Values. Nonetheless, this is a different type of measuring. This type requires less effort, but is just as impactful.

Definitions.

The way we define things in life have a profound effect on how we see ourselves and others. Let's look at the table of Values from Chapter One, Figure 1.2.

Authenticity	Achievement	Adventure	Authority	Autonomy
Balance	Beauty	Boldness	Compassion	Challenge
Citizenship	Community	Competency	Contribution	Creativity
Curiosity	Determination	Fairness	Faith	Fame
Friendship	Fun	Growth	Happiness	Honesty
Humor	Influence	Harmony	Justice	Kindness
Knowledge	Leadership	Learning	Love	Loyalty
Openness	Optimism	Peace	Pleasure	Poise
Popularity	Purpose	Recognition	Religion	Reputation
Respect	Responsibility	Security	Self Respect	Service
Spirituality	Stability	Success	Status	Trust
Vision	Wealth	Well-Being	Wisdom	Zen

As you read each item, you instantly understand what it means. Moreover, if asked, you can quickly assess yourself or another person on the degree to which they represent a certain value. For instance, "openness" to me is defined as an outgoing personality that is often observed sharing ideas and opinions and is quick to answer questions honestly. I consider myself fairly open, about a 6 out of 10, but one of my friends is more open than I am. He is a solid 8. To try and work on improving my own rating, I will share with you that it was not until I provided this example that I looked up "openness" in the dictionary to see the actual definition. I overlooked the part of "openness" that talks about free access to information. The Internet is a great example of an open information sharing space. By rushing myself through the exercise, I did not think about access to information as a part of "openness."

To further illustrate the importance of accurate and thorough definitions, I will share my recollection of a meeting that occurred last year. I was invited to talk to a small group of professionals from the wealth management, insurance, legal, information technology, and senior living fields. After a brief introduction, I asked what the word "motivation" meant to each person in the room. Everyone provided great responses. I then asked one person who was checking his smartphone during the presentation to look up a definition and to read it out loud. One of the words that he read was "reason." None of the participants mentioned it prior. A brief silence at first was quickly filled with a lively discussion. As a takeaway, all agreed that nodding during an exchange of trivial terms does not necessarily mean an agreement upon their definitions. Think about that the next time you get a nod when talking to others.

Over the past quarter century, I have witnessed several misconceptions, stereotypes, or myths that have taken roots in our culture and influenced our Values and Beliefs. In turn, Values and Beliefs drive our Actions, such as thinking. There is hardly a day that goes by without a mention of these stereotypes, either by the media or by people with whom I may have a conversation. In this chapter I discuss and analyze several of these myths. As always, my intent is to raise awareness and provide information for you to consider.

"Most people use only 10% of their brain."

Do not feel bad if you believe this. It is a widespread myth among many highly educated professionals world-wide! It all started in the early 20th century and had do to with the psychological works on intellectual potential of an average person. Originally, the conclusion was that an average person uses 10% of their intellectual potential. Over time, one misinterpretation led to another and before long, the "10% of intellectual capacity" turned into "10% of the brain." After Albert Einstein's name was used in association with "10% of the brain," the longevity of the myth was secured.

Today, clinical neurologists and neuropsychologists conclude that losing 10% or 20% of any parts of the brain due to trauma or disease leaves a patient with a serious deficiency in conscious awareness. Moreover, many procedures implemented during routine neurosurgeries showed that our brain has no "silent areas" waiting to be awoken. Occasionally, a part of the brain is unused due to injury or disease. That part of the brain will either become unusable matter or the areas nearby will take over that part of the brain to support the existing functions. Either way, the unused part does not remain idle for long. Using fMRI and other advanced electronic equipment, the scientists were able to map out the areas of the brain that are responsible for various tasks. These studies have not discovered any dormant areas, and even simple tasks generally required involvement of processing centers spread throughout the whole brain.

The myth has a natural appeal of an enormous, 90% additional potential for our brains, if only we knew how to tap into it. It is hard to let go. However, there is no substitute to time, commitment, and hard work to improve one's mental abilities. If debunking the brain myth is disappointing to some, the good news is that there is little limitation on personal and professional improvement.

"The left brain is different from right brain."

"However tempting it is to talk of right and left hemispheres in isolation, they are actually two half-brains, designed to work together as

a smooth, single, integrated whole in one entire, complete brain. The left hemisphere knows how to handle logic and the right hemisphere knows about the world. Put the two together and one gets a powerful thinking machine. Use either on its own and the result can be bizarre or absurd." — Chris McManus.[1]

The reality is that unless one undergoes a "split brain" operation, both hemispheres are involved in performing the tasks at hand. It just so happens that one hemisphere is slightly better at some processes than the other. Therefore, one hemisphere will do the part that it can do faster than the other, yet both will be simultaneously involved. For example, as a trained musician, not only did I get emotionally involved while listening to music, I can also tell what instruments are used, and depending on the complexity, can replicate the parts each instrument plays with some degree of accuracy. If at the moment of intense listening I was connected to an fMRI, the image would show a high level of activity in both of my hemispheres. My confidence in saying this is supported by works of Mike Aamodt, Qi Wang, and Sergio Della Sala, to name a few. Admittedly, reading such works is boring compared to the excitement of highly advertised, pseudo-scientific, "right brain" training of various kinds and price tags.

Think about a time when you were making an emotional purchase while making a logical justification for it. Hardly any tasks are exclusively "left brain" or "right brain." Depending on your situation as well as your cultural background and social skills, as opposed to some physiological deficiency of your right hemisphere, you may show more emotions or get more creative. Remember, at this very moment you are your best. You are fully equipped to make the best decision based on what you know.

"Subliminal messages have real power."

Have you ever heard of a subliminal entrepreneur? The term refers to the idea that listening to music mixed with subliminal messages can help you become successful. If you think that this is a thing of the past, take a moment and search the web. You will find various products that can be purchased on CDs or downloaded as MP3 files. Some products are sold for hundreds of dollars.

Defined as "below the levels detectable by our sensory systems," the subliminal messages must be simple but "loud" enough to compete with normal stimulus for our brain and nervous system to receive and process. Therefore, in theory, one has to be exposed to subliminal messages for some period of time to be influenced by them. But why do messages have to be subliminal? The subliminal entrepreneurs will tell you that these signals can encode the subconscious mind with the desired messages that will subsequently elicit the desired behavior.

The importance of the subconscious mind was made popular by the works of Freud. Most scientific psychologists have long abandoned the once popular theories of the human subconscious. A repeatable experiment with a high probability of a predetermined outcome is one example of admissible scientific evidence. In other words, if listening to subliminal recordings had a 10%, 20%, or 50% repeatable success rate, and it was the content of the recording that was proved to cause the results, one could argue the point. However, in several scientific experiments it was shown that priming, or the suggestive language used by the scientists, made the test subjects believe they were getting better even when the recordings were originally made for encoding the subconscious for a completely different goal. This is known as an illusory placebo effect. Test subjects did not improve, but they thought they did. The power of subliminal messages is largely a myth.

I did use the qualifier "largely" because there is something about this subject that does affect our thoughts and behaviors.

It is the use of the priming in conjunction with the messages, i.e. advertising that can be effective. However, priming has a very short-term effect and cannot encode our minds. Nevertheless, during important conversations, where an immediate decision is made, choosing your worlds wisely is not a bad idea. Silence is also a good alternative.

How can we avoid the emotional component when making a buying decision? We can't. If we were to try, we would be fighting against two things. First, we all have the complex and ever-changing psychological factors that drive our decisions. Second, billions are spent annually in advertising to influence our decisions. Keep a budget and record your spending. Analyze your decision making pattern and be better prepared next time.

"Low self-esteem leads to violence."

Self-esteem is defined as a subjective emotional evaluation of self-worth. It is also a judgment and attitude towards self. This is one loaded definition that is prone to confusion and misinterpretation. The validity and methodology of several dozen of tests to measure one's self-esteem often comes into question within the science of psychology. Some tests have stood the test of time better than others. Self-esteem is a complicated matter and should be treated with respect.

To investigate whether or not low self-esteem is a cause of violence, a series of interesting experiments were conducted. The first step of the experiment was to evaluate the participant's level of self-esteem. The responses ranged from low to very high. Those who scored extremely high were called narcissists. During the second step, the participants were asked to write essays expressing their attitudes towards abortion. A research assistant disguised as another participant evaluated each essay. The evaluations were randomly assigned without the assistant reading the essays. Half of them got positive comments that said "No suggestions, great essay!" while the other half received comments that said "This is the worst essay I have ever read!" In the final step of the experiment, the participants were asked to retaliate against their evaluators with a loud noise. The narcissists used far louder noises than the other participants. Positive evaluations produced no such effect. This series of experiments, and similar ones that followed, revealed a peculiar trend that led to the following conclusion. Violence, whether in teens or in adults, is caused by two factors. First, an individual's perceived *high* self-esteem. In fact, many narcissists believe in having special privileges because of their perceived superiority over others. The second factor is the presence of a certain circumstance that would challenge the individual's perceived worth.

History has many examples of individuals and groups whose superior views of themselves, when given access to real political power and economic resources, culminated in military aggression like wars and revolutions.

"Most people experience a midlife crisis."

Merriam-Webster defines midlife crisis as "a period of emotional turmoil in middle age characterized especially by a strong desire for change." As an example, the dictionary offers "we knew he was going through a midlife crisis when he bought a new sports car."[2] It is very common to think of a man in the context of this subject matter. Thanks to the movie industry, middle age men have been depicted in many movies going through the crisis. Often, these depictions are inaccurate.

When I approached my mid-30s, I experienced a strong desire to change. The changes that eventually took place did not include what we would typically associate with a midlife crisis like marrying a younger woman, buying a sports car, or changing my career. Nevertheless, some of my friends used the term to explain the reason why I would eat healthier or exercise regularly, for instance. The choices I've made came from the inside. I was connecting my new Values with Actions. Ultimately, changes in Actions made me who I am today.

Looking at the two words, midlife and crisis, separately offers some additional insights. The Free Dictionary defines midlife as "the period in a person's life from about age 40 to about age 60."[3] The middle is pushed towards the more senior side. However, risk of a divorce, one of the most common elements associated with a midlife crisis, is higher for men and women below 40 years of age.

Next, let's check the causality within the definition of midlife crisis. It seems counter intuitive that a desire to change causes crisis. Change is widely praised in business, corporate, and social arenas, and is generally recognized as a sign of progress. I believe change is a proactive measure against the crisis. Let's try this causality in reverse. Can crisis cause the desire for change? Crisis is defined by Merriam-Webster as "an unstable or crucial time or state of affairs in which a decisive change is impending."[4] Whether the change is either the aftermath of the crisis (i.e. property values drop after a real estate crisis) or the way to deal with crisis (i.e. changes in comprehensive macroeconomic strategy to mitigate the effects of inflation), the crisis does appear to cause change. While the definition is not a total failure of logic, the exercise of caution is a wise choice. The term midlife crisis itself is about 40 - 45 years old, and is undergoing its own scrutiny by the subject matter experts.

Third, the premise that most people experience the midlife crisis is definitely a myth. According to one large study of over 7,000 men and women aged 25 to 74, people in the 40 to 60 age range generally felt more in control of their lives.[5] 75% of respondents rated their relationships as good to excellent and the remaining 25% do not automatically fall into the midlife crisis group. Once again, first divorces, a major sign of a midlife crisis, usually occur when men and women are in their early to mid-30s. That is about a decade prior to entering the midlife range.

Is there such a thing as a midlife crisis after all? Of course there is. The best way to look at any personal crisis is to view it as a compilation of certain factors that make everyday life no longer enjoyable or meaningful. Over a period of time, all values come into question and some are determined to be no longer serving one's life. But this is not a crisis yet. While everyone's tipping point is different, it is not until a person starts acting in a new way that we call it a crisis. Additionally, the new behaviors, driven by a new sets of values, would have to have a profound effect on one's life, career, relationships, and so forth. The good news is some of the changes can be positive. Newfound meaning in one's career, a new business pursuit, and going back to school for an advanced degree are all typical examples of a midlife crisis's aftermath. As to the relationships, some will survive the crisis and some will not. A new vision may or may not be shared and supported by a partner.

Finally, according to many studies in the US, the midlife crisis happens to only about 8% - 10% of men and women age 40 to 60. While 10% of hundreds of millions of adults is a large number, it is a far cry from the 51% required to use the word "most."

"Human memory is like a tape recorder."

Many studies conducted in the past decades have revealed that about 35% - 55% of students and professional psychotherapists think that memory operates like a tape recorder and the memories are fixed in the mind. It is also believed that these memories reside undisturbed in the subconscious, not affected by the passage of time or more recent memories that may compete for space. This is a myth. The fact is that time plays a big factor in the accuracy of memory retrieval. Studies have shown that people going through emotionally charged events tend to change the description of the event when interviewed in as little as 12-18 months. The way the interview is conducted and the way the questions are asked will also affect the respondents' answers.

You may wonder if the accuracy of memory recollection is important since in business dealings we rely on signed and dated documents. Often, these documents are also witnessed and notarized for added protection against fraud. In everyday life, we rely on the Internet to check facts, confirm reservations, remind us about scheduled meetings, and even to watch movies of family gatherings recorded on smartphones and uploaded to social media. Technology offers us a great system that would help accurately recollect the details of the past. While this is true, if you happen to be called on as an eyewitness during a criminal investigation, the details of your recollection can make a difference in the life of a person being charged.

Elizabeth Loftus is an American cognitive psychologist specializing in human memory for the past four decades. In her June 2013 TED lecture in Edinburg, Scotland, Elizabeth made these very important points: [6]

- Many people, including jurors, believe that memory works like a recording device. Once information is gathered, it can be accurately "played back" at any time. This is not true. She says: "Memory works like a Wikipedia page. You can go in and change it, but so can other people."

- The deliberate word choice, or insinuation influences our memories. When an eyewitness is led with questioning that aims to change his or her disposition, the eyewitness may provide an inaccurate account of the events. As a result, an innocent person may be convicted and put away for a long period of time.

- Based on experiments, a false memory can be planted in our minds and it can affect our behavior. For instance, a memory of getting sick after eating certain foods resulted in participants avoiding these foods after the study. Additionally, positive memories associated with a consumption of vegetables, once planted, resulted in participants wanting to eat more vegetables.

"Handwriting reveals personality."

Have you ever tried to read your doctor's handwriting on a prescription or referral slip? In doing so, have you made certain assumptions about your doctor's character based on the handwriting? If so, you have played a role of a graphologist, a specialist that studies physical characteristics and patterns of handwritings as the means to ascertain the writer's psychological state or personality traits. Conceived in the 17th century in Italy, graphology has grown over time. In the US, the International Graphoanalysis Society, or IGAS, at its peak, had about 10,000 members. This privately held corporation has recently gone through a bankruptcy and it is hard to infer its financial viability based on the look of their website, www.igas.com. Graphologist, in the US, is a legitimate job, in the fields of an employment profiling, psychological analysis, marital compatibility, medical diagnosis, and graphotherapy.

Graphology is based on these four beliefs:

- Writing is a form of expressive movement, so it reflects our personalities.

- Handwriting is brainwriting.

- Writing is individualized and personality is unique, so they must reflect each other.

- Graphology is useful in selecting employees.

The fallacy of the first belief is that the relationship between body language, as an indicator of one's temperament, and one's handwriting, as an extension of a body language or gestures is weak.

If you were to write your signature using your foot, with a pencil between your toes, it will look like your real signature. In the name of science, I tried it. I got an even better result by using the big toe and writing on the sand. While this experiment proves that the writing is controlled by our brains rather than limbs, so are other functions, like sneezing, for instance. Believing that writing is a function of the brain, while true, does not offer correlation between handwriting and personality traits.

The third belief is based on idiosyncrasy. Faces on driving licenses are unique as well, but tell us nothing about one's ability to drive safely. It is also important to clarify that a Graphologists is not a Questioned Document Examiner (QDE), a specialist that assesses the authenticity of handwritten documents for historians or courts. Interestingly, the QDEs say nothing about personality traits of the writer.

Finally, the use of graphology in personnel selection has two major flaws. First, graphologists get many relative clues in the content of the handwritten document. This includes previous employment and criminal records. These clues are good predictors of future job performance. The second flaw is the fact that due to cost consideration, graphologists often examine the handwriting of the applicants that were already pre-screened and now are going through a final selection. This process makes it impossible to see if anyone who was screened out would do better based solely on the recommendation of a graphologist.

Scientific support of graphology is nearly non-existent. In one study, the participants were asked to write the same text to eliminate any clues about their personality but the handwriting.

The task of the graphologists was to predict job performance. The graphologists did no better than chance at predicting job performance. A meta-analysis over 200 studies, conducted by Geoffrey Dean, failed to support graphology as a scientific way of detecting personality traits and predicting job performance.[7]

Public acceptance of graphology's merit can be attributed to two factors. The first factor is representativeness heuristics. For example, when we see a man in a ski mask with a gun running out of the bank, chances are we are witnessing a bank robbery and not a motion picture production of it. However, in the case of graphology, statements like "upward slant in handwriting indicates the uplifted or optimistic personality" do not stand the test of studies. The second factor is The Barnum Effect, which is easily experienced if you were to read your horoscope. Passages that are supposedly unique to your birthday are universal. The effect was illustrated by Bertram R. Forer in 1948. In a study, Forer gave each student in the study group a card that described their personality. Each student was asked to rate the card on the scale from 0 (very poor) to 5 (excellent) on how well the card described their personality. The average rating was a 4.26, while each card contained the same 12 sentences. Below are some sentences from the cards: [8]

- Disciplined and self-controlled outside, you tend to be worrisome and insecure inside.

- At times you have serious doubts as to whether you have made the right decision or done the right thing.

- Security is one of your major goals in life.

- You pride yourself as an independent thinker and do not accept others' statements without satisfactory proof.

While the first three expression can easily be attributable to all, the forth one is harder to argue due to its personal appeal. However, this statement may not reflect the reality. Some people, indeed, accept statements of others without proof.

"Happiness is all about money, health, and relationships."

In the 1990s, I heard so many motivational speakers it was impossible not to see a pattern. What emerged was a formula for happiness that was embedded in their presentations. It was assumed that everyone was looking for money, health, and relationships. Today, the emotional appeal to wealth, health, and relationships are still being used in marketing. With the help of social scientists, let's examine if money, health, and relationships cause higher levels of happiness.

Money.

It goes without saying that a certain amount of money must be earned or received by other means to allow for a person's survival. The amount does vary based on location, family size, and other factors. That said, I invite you to take a look and think about the two exhibits that follow. First, depicted in Figure 7.1, are test results of a 2010 study conducted by Kahneman and Deaton.[9]

Fig. 7.1

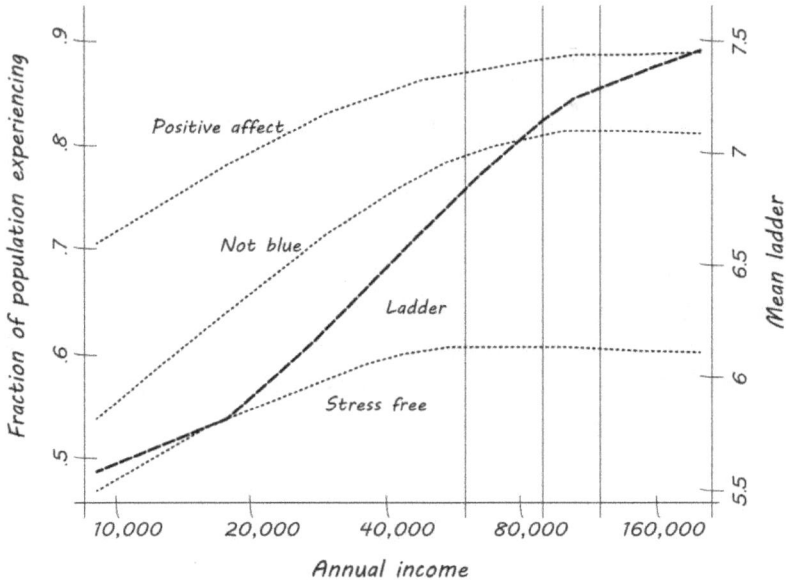

Positive affect is the average of the fractions of the population reporting happiness. "Not blue" is 1 minus the average of the fractions of the population reporting worry and sadness. "Stress free" is the fraction of the population who did not report stress. These measures are marked on the left hand side. The ladder is the average reported number on a scale of 0 to 10, marked on the right hand side. According to this study, individuals receiving $75,000 - $120,000 in annual income have not reported higher levels of happiness, as an emotional component.

Second, is a study by Diener and Silegman encompassing wide income brackets in different locations.[10] Figure 7.2 on the following page depicts the result of that study.

Fig. 7.2

Life Satisfaction for Various Groups

Group	Rating
Forbes magazine's "richest Americans"	5.8
Pennsylvania Amish	5.8
Inughuit (Inuit people in northerrn Greenland)	5.8
African Maasai	5.7
International college-student sample (47 nations in 2000.)	4.9
Illinois Amish	4.9
Calcutta slum dwellers	4.6
Fresno, California, homeless	2.9
Calcutta pavement dwellers (homeless)	2.9

Note: Respondents indicated their agreement with the statement "You are satisfied with your life" using a scale from 1 (complete disagreement) to 7 (complete agreement); 4 is neutral rating.

Evidently, the 400 richest Americans are as satisfied with their life as the Maasai of East Africa. The Maasai live in huts with no electricity or running water and make their living by herding. Even the slum dwellers of Calcutta show above the neutral point on the rating scale. This suggests that luxuries are not a requirement for happiness.

Money is a relatively new part of the history of the human race. It has only been around for about 4,500 years. Before that, a trade of goods for services, sometimes referred to as barter, was common among strangers and gift-giving was practiced within a closer community. Consumption was limited to what the community could build, farm, and hunt. Fundamentally, human activities were not that different from higher animals. Some animals show behavior that can be considered as gift-giving or barter. With the introduction of a state, the concept of money takes hold and allows for a wealth accumulation that was never seen before.

Behavioral economics as a branch of economics uses psychology to explain human behavior as it relates to financial decision making. It is a complicated process and involves factors like culture, cognition, and emotions to name a few. Behavioral economics is a fascinating field; however, I will stop at its acknowledgement and an invitation to explore more on your own.

Health.

Are happy people healthier? Does good health lead to happiness? While the causality goes both ways, there are some important distinctions. First, there are objective reports of physical health by medical professionals and there are self-reports. Both show positive correlation between good health and emotional well-being. Even when physical health, objectively reported, is less than perfect, a person's ability to adapt over time is the key to emotional well-being. That said, illnesses that significantly limit one's ability to function are mostly self-reported and show strong correlation with predicted longevity. Nevertheless, as Diener and Silegman point out: "Thus, well-being and absence of ill-being predict better later health, but the mixed nature of the data indicates that the association between well-being and physical health is influenced by variables that are not yet understood."[11]

There is also evidence that happiness positively affects health. Numerous studies in the past three decades have shown that patients that are emotionally more positive live longer and recover quicker compared with patients that are anxious or depressed. As we have seen in Chapter Six, optimism helps to avoid post-partum depression and can even reduce the risk of developing heart disease. In one study, psychological support was given to ten cancer patients that were in emotional distress. Five showed benefits from the intervention. None of the ten showed any adverse effects. Furthermore, happiness helps us to cope with chronic pain and manage blood pressure when in distress. While the mechanism behind physiological improvements is sometimes unclear, the amount of evidence clearly supports happiness and emotional well-being as a cause.

Relationships.

Compared to money and health, one arguably has less control over their own relationship situation. Great long-term relationships take commitment from two people. Does the hard work of staying in a relationship pay off in terms of a person's happiness level? Let's take a look at the data below. Figure 7.3 shows the percentage of married adults in the US who answered their marriage was "very happy."[12]

Fig. 7.3

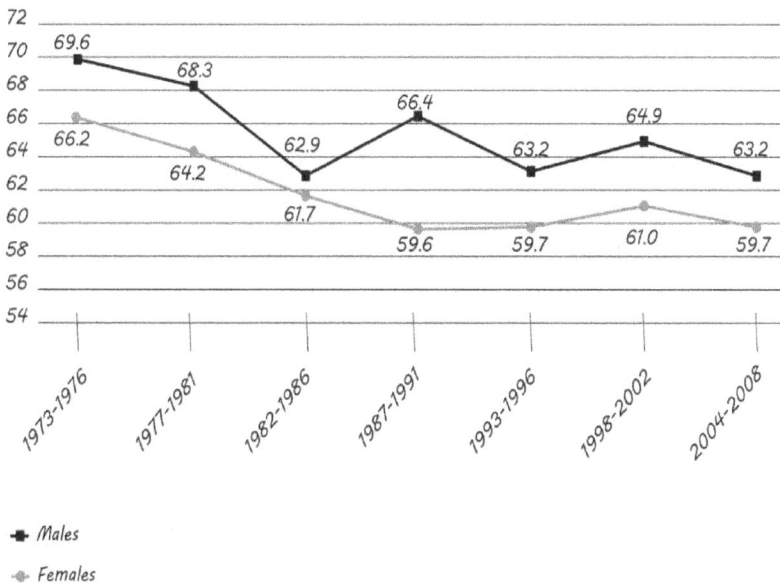

- Males
- Females

According to the same source, the University of Chicago's General Social Survey, "unhappily married adults who divorced or separated were no happier, on average, than unhappily married adults who stayed married. Even unhappy spouses who had divorced and remarried were no happier, on average, than unhappy spouses who stayed married. This was true even after controlling for race, age, gender, and income."

If happiness does not have strong ties to money, health, or relationships, where does it come from? Biologically speaking, we all feel happy when four hormones are released in our bodies. The hormones are dopamine, serotonin, endorphins, and oxytocin. Below are general descriptions of each hormone and tips on how you can try to boost their levels.

- Dopamine is a pleasure hormone that is often associated with striving and achieving goals. It helps us stay focused and alert. Some of the ways to boost dopamine is to set daily or weekly goals and work towards them. We get a dopamine boost when we check stuff off a list physically. Exercise is also a great way to increase your dopamine level.

- Serotonin regulates mood, prevents anxiety and depression, and makes us happy and sociable. Recalling happy memories and eating foods like eggs, cheese, nuts, and salmon helps increase your serotonin level. Low-intensity workouts also help.

- There are many kinds of endorphins and they act in different ways. Endorphins are best known as natural pain killers and for their ability to reduce anxiety. There is a variety of things we can do to boost endorphins in our bodies including eating spicy food, walking 30 minutes a day, or spending time in a sauna.

- Oxytocin is sometimes called the love hormone. It has been associated with social behavior and closeness between two or more people in a variety of situations. Additional benefits of oxytocin are its ability to protect the heart against stress. Physical closeness like touching, hugging, massages and sex help release oxytocin. My favorite work that integrates the effects of oxytocin with the professional arena is a book *Conversational Intelligence* by Judith Glaser. The types of conversations we are engaged in at work not only vary, but often reflect on the overall culture of our work environment. By changing the conversation, a company can change its culture. Oxytocin plays a crucial role in the conversational intelligence model, but I can't give it all away. You should read the book for yourself.

After this long list of myths and semi-truths, let me bring you back to where we left off. Measurements, stemming out of our Beliefs and Values, often come in a form of opinions or judgements. They are more subjective compared to Measurements of Actions discussed previously in Chapter Four and can be observed, for instance, in how we manage our personal expectations.

Expectation Management.

There are two schools of beliefs when it comes to how high to set the expectation bar relative to our anticipated future. The first suggests that we should keep our expectations of being happy or successful low and, should the future fail to bring us happiness or success, we won't get disappointed. We get what we expected. The second school of thought says that we should set our expectations high because doing so will psych us up and we will do better. Even if some will fail, they will not be any worse off than those who accepted lower expectations of themselves. Expectations are always forward-looking; therefore, they provide hope for a better tomorrow.

When we measure our risks prior to making important decisions like getting married, we might disregard the fact that in the US, depending on the source, the divorce rate ranges from 40% to 50%. Optimists will be 100% sure that they belong to the other 50% to 60%, while the pessimists may not even consider getting married.

A good expectation management system is a combination of having true knowledge and a structure that will allow forward movement in case things don't work out on the first or second try. We may call it optimism, faith, or a contingency plan. As long as we keep moving towards the desired future, achieving happiness and success will always seem possible.

When expecting a certain behavior from others, we should start with a clear understanding of the other person's Beliefs and Values. If different from our own, the Beliefs and Values may provide good reasons for a different way of thinking and acting. Just because someone does not conduct themselves in the manner we expect, we should not be too quick to judge, or measure someone's actions with our own moral ruler. I find it fascinating how often I am wrong when I try and guess someone's motives for saying or doing certain things. It is through conversation and getting to know another person that I get to see a situation through their eyes. When I do, their worlds or actions make perfect sense.

Chapter Summary.

Subjective measurements stem out from our Beliefs and Values and show up as opinions and judgements of self and others that often are based on myths and half-truths. We saw some examples of the most common misconceptions. My goal is not to change the Beliefs and Values of my readers, but to show that there might be another reality. We don't always know what is true or false; therefore, we have to make assumptions and take some risks.

In pursuit of happiness, it might be helpful to keep a biological perspective and take notice of situations that most often cause the release of dopamine, serotonin, endorphins, and oxytocin. While you will not be able to see them, you will feel the effects of the hormones.

Chapter Eight: Feelings and Emotions.

You may have noticed that there was hardly any in-depth discussion of feelings and emotions thus far. In Chapter One, we saw them as invisible Actions that are very hard to control. (Figure 1.5) There were some other brief mentions in other chapters. As the result of such a limited scope of discussion, the Model seems a bit mechanical and does not fully reflect the human nature of the readers it aims to help.

I have purposely delayed elaborating on feelings and emotions so that I can dedicate an entire chapter to the topic. The subject matter is way more than some Actions, lurking in the shadows, or spinning out of control. They, in fact, can be quite visible. Additionally, not only can we observe our feelings and emotions and understand their origin, there are ways to achieve mastery in terms of just how much we let our feelings and emotions control our lives. For starters, I'd like to share a personal story.

It is hard to forget a conversation that took place about over ten years ago between me and my daughter. Katherine was four-and-a-half-years-old. After dinner, she suddenly disappeared. I found her in her room sitting on the floor, sobbing. "Why are you crying?" I asked, stretching out my vowels. She did not reply. "Did you fall and hurt yourself?" I kept going. "No, Daddy, I did not fall," she whispered. "Then why are you crying?" I persisted, thinking I outsmarted her again. This tricky question had always worked in the past. "Because you hurt my feelings!" she exclaimed. This was the first time I heard my daughter utter the word "feelings." My own feelings got mixed up. On one hand, I was upset with myself for what I had done. On the other hand, I realized that my daughter was no longer a little baby. For the first time she was able to clearly express her emotional side. Pride and joy filled my heart as I stretched my arms to give her a big hug. I also kissed her cheek and apologized. From that moment on, I've never talked to Katherine in parentese.

Feelings and Emotions: The Model Redefined.

Perhaps, it would be better to compare feelings and emotions with air inside the tires than to call them invisible Actions. The reason for that is the fact that the Wheels make contact with the road through tires. Depending on the type of the vehicle and the road surface, air pressure plays an important role. For instance, wider tires and lower inflation pressure usually means better mobility in snow, ice, and sand. The technology that allowed changing the amount of air inside the tires of military and other special vehicles has been around since the 1950s. Similarly to the overinflated tires spinning freely in deep snow, strong feelings and emotions can cause us to get stuck in the moment.

Within the Model, feelings and emotions are present in all Wheels. Let's consider a few possibilities. In the Beliefs and Values Wheel, the acceptable amount of visible feelings and emotions are determined by cultural norms. For example, in Western society, it is customary for men to show less feelings and emotions compared to women. In the Wheel of Goals, SMART criteria alone can connote either positively or negatively based on how we feel about the Goals we are pursuing. We can easily get misguided by thinking that pursuing SMART goals makes us smart and not having goals that fit the criteria is a sign of mental weakness. Experiencing certain feelings and emotions inside while trying to maintain a calm appearance and keeping visible Actions aligned with the other three Wheels is the challenge of the Wheel of Actions. Finally, in the Wheel of Measurements, feelings and emotions could run high or low depending on the grade, job review, self-assessment, and so forth. I invite you to think about other examples of feelings and emotions manifesting within the Model.

Separating feelings from emotions.

In the science of psychology, there are four schools of thought. The first school defines feelings the same way as emotions and uses the words interchangeably. The second school believes that feelings are certain types of emotions that are tied to a particular object. The third school divides feelings into lower and higher level categories and lists feelings together with emotions and affections to describe emotional states. The fourth school separates feeling and emotions. In doing so, a framework that is more clear and consistent compared to the other three emerges. Figure 8.1 summarizes some basic differences.

Fig. 8.1

	EMOTIONS	FEELINGS
EVOLUTIONAL ORIGINS	Developed earlier and attributed to animals and humans	Developed later and attributed mostly to humans
DURATION	Highly situational, short-term, providing intangible significance to "here and now"	Related to an object, stable, and long-term
COEXISTENCE	Same emotions are found in different feelings	Same feelings are found in different emotions

Emotions.

What used to be a hypothesis before, the notion that higher animals possess emotions has been substantiated by decades of research and recent findings. One of the most notable works on emotions in the field of neuroscience were conducted by Jaak Panksepp. Additionally, a research paper written in 2015 by scientists from University of Michigan, University of Oxford, and University of Aarhus uses brain scans of rats, monkeys, and newborn babies.[1]

The study raises a question of whether or not the evidence of pleasure, displeasure, and some other emotions can be found in a neuronal circuitry of test subjects. The outcome of the experiments was successful. Advanced fMRI imagery provided enough evidence to call certain areas of animal and human brain "causal." Not only did these areas react in a predictable and measurable way to various outside stimuli, but when stimulated directly, body language responses were the same. For example, when sugar was given to rats, monkeys, and human babies, their facial expressions where visually similar and included relaxed and slightly opened lips. In all three types of brains, the same areas would show up as "hot spots" in response to sugar. When "hot spots" were stimulated directly via electrodes, all test subjects' facial expressions were as if they were tasting sugar with their tongues. When a bitter taste was introduced, all subjects' facial expressions resembled crying to signal "disgust." Areas of the brains that corresponded to bitter taste were also similar in all brain structures. Direct stimulation of disgust hot spots yielded similar facial expressions. The significance of these findings is enormous as they help to support the claim that certain emotions in animals and human are objective. In other words, no subjective interpretations that require higher level of brain functioning are needed to show positive or negative emotions.

When we are talking about a developed human brain, such as that of a healthy individual with normal educational and social upbringing, the emotions will be subjective. These emotions may be simple or complex, but they will represent subjective interpretations of an event. The process of interpreting is so fast that it does not register as thinking; however, the process is always there. The filter through which the interpretation occurs can be any of the Four Wheels of the

Model. Any events can be seen as information about Beliefs, Goals, Actions, or Measurements. (Figure 8.2)

Fig. 8.2

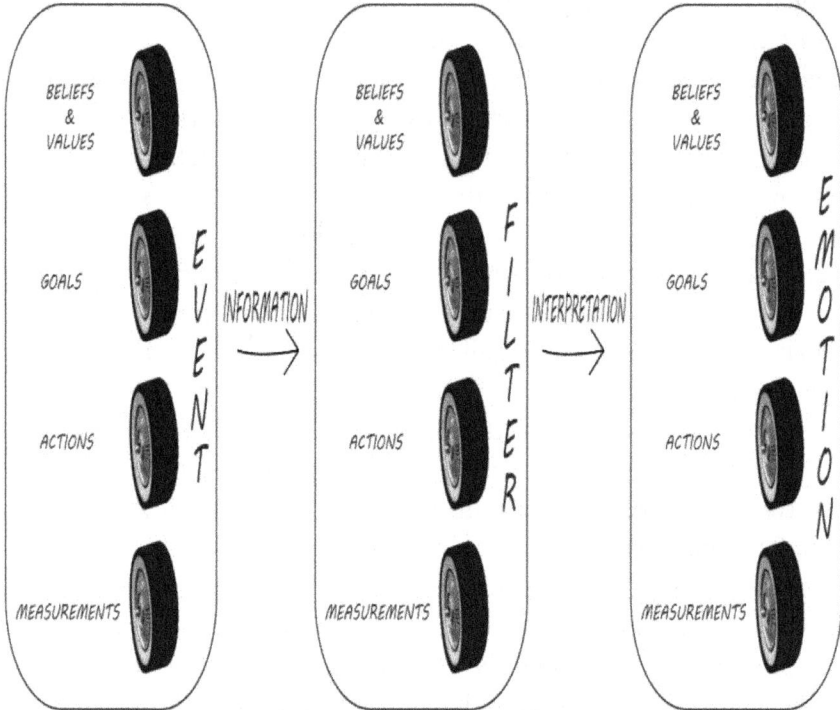

This is a generalized, non-scientific representation of subjective emotional reaction to an event combined with the Wheels of the Model. This is just an entertaining visual. Feel free to add a few arrows of your own that could show additional relationship between the depicted parts.

As an awareness of a variety of views on basic emotions selected theorists for the past century, Ortony and Turner put together a table that has been replicated and updated in Figure 8.3. [2]

Fig. 8.3

THEORIST	BASIC EMOTIONS
Plutchik	Acceptance, anger, anticipation, disgust, joy, fear, sadness, surprise
Arnold	Anger, aversion, courage, dejection, desire, despair, fear, hate, hope, love, sadness
Ekman, Friesen, and Ellsworth	Anger, disgust, fear, joy, sadness, surprise
Frijda	Desire, happiness, interest, surprise, wonder, sorrow
Gray	Rage and terror, anxiety, joy
Izard	Anger, contempt, disgust, distress, fear, guilt, interest, joy, shame, surprise
James	Fear, grief, love, rage
McDougall	Anger, disgust, elation, fear, subjection, tender-emotion, wonder
Mowrer	Pain, pleasure
Oatley and Johnson-Laird	Anger, disgust, anxiety, happiness, sadness
Panksepp*	**Seeking, rage, fear, lust, care, grief, play**
Tomkins	Anger, interest, contempt, disgust, distress, fear, joy, shame, surprise
Watson	Fear, love, rage
Weiner and Graham	Happiness, sadness

*In pre-1990 works, Panksepp's talked about four basic emotions: expectancy, fear, rage, and panic. From the late 1990s, his framework includes seven basic emotions listed above.

Arbitrarily, I have chosen to focus on the current works of Jaak Panksepp. Figure 8.4 provides a summary of Panksepp's view of basic and emergent emotions as well as emotional disorders. Note an addition of Self system and its application.[3] Plus and minus signs indicate whether or not emotion is positive or negative, or both.

Fig 8.4

Basic Emotional System	Emergent Emotions	Emotional Disorders
SEEKING (+&-)	Interest Frustration Craving	Obssesive Compulsive Paranoid Schizophrenia Addictive Personalities
RAGE (-&+)	Anger Irritability Contempt Hatred	Aggression Psychopathic tendencies Personality Disorders
FEAR (-)	Simple anxiety Worry Psychic trauma	Generalized Anxiety Disorders Phobias PTSD variants
PANIC (-)	Separation distress Sadness Guilt/Shame Shyness Embarrassment	Panic Attacks Pathological Grief Depression Agoraphobia Social Phobias
PLAY (+)	Joy and glee Happy playfulness	Mania ADHD
LUST (+&-)	Erotic feelings Jealousy	Fetishes Sexual Addictions
CARE (+)	Nurturance Love Attraction	Dependency Disorders Autistic aloofness Attachment Disorders
The SELF - a substrate for Core Consciousness	A mechanism for all emotional feelings	Multiple Personality Disorders?

Awareness of various emotions, aside from satisfying basic curiosity, have limited value if left without a discussion regarding their functions. Hard to imagine that just a few decades ago the two dominating thoughts regarding functions of emotions were a) emotions have no functions and b) emotions used to serve functions that are no longer needed. Nevertheless, works of Carroll Izard and others propose a useful perspective on functions of emotions. Let's take a closer look.

According to Izard and Ackerman[4], our emotions serve three functions: motivational, organizational, and regulatory. Refer to Figure 8.3 to see the list of emotions Izard considered basic. Motivational function is close to goals and behavior.

Organizational function is responsible for cognition and actions. Regulatory process is a bridge that connects situations with the way we respond emotionally and physically. The process includes the situation, its appraisal, and the actual emotional response. In a way, regulatory process can be depicted by Figure 8.2. Yet, the process is a complex one and can involve several emotions of various magnitudes as a response to the situation.

While the question of usefulness of emotions is still debatable among emotion theorists, I don't think we can just turn our emotions off should we deem them useless. Therefore, let's assume some practicality of having emotions and look at specific examples. (Figure 8.5)

Fig. 8.5

Emotion	Usage
Interest	1. Promotes exploration and learning. Requires involvment of consciousness. Thus, plays important role in adaptation. 2. Motivates energy mobilization for focus, engagement, and interaction.
Joy/Happiness	1. Promotes social interaction which leads to bonding. Bonding is essential between a parent and an offspring during early development. 2. Helps to cope with stress. 3. Expression of joy through smile is a universal sign for a friendly interaction.
Sadness	1. Similar to Joy increases social bond. 2. Grief, the related emotion, helps a group to get over death together and increases chances of group's survival. 3. Slows down cognitive and motor functions which helps to focus on issue or to gain a new perspective.
Anger	1. Prevents aggression and fighting when expressed by a stronger opponent. 2. Increases and maintains higher level of energy.
Shame	1. Motivates social conformity. 2. Promotes self-awareness. A person may feel inappropriate or inadequate.
Fear	1. Promotes avoidance behavior. 2. Stimulates perceptual and cognitive processes.

Experiencing one emotion may trigger another. For instance, interest may motivate exploration of a new city or a country. During travel, while interest is still dominant, unknown places and strangers met along the way may trigger fear. Joy and sadness may occur at the same time, resulting in "tears of joy."

In one of more recent works by Greek scientists, positive emotions like love, joy, and interest, were first identified, as they have been previously, to have three broader functions that include the following:[5]

- Broadening individual's perspectives, figuratively and literally to include "wider visual search patterns," makes one more social and flexible in goal setting.

- Increasing in psychological capacity to offset the effects of negative emotions.

- Leading, ultimately, to well-being.

Second, a sample that included 11,422 Greek adults from 18 to 83 years of age were given tests over a period of several years. The results collected were measured effects of positive and negative emotions along the following scales:

- Subjective Happiness

- Life Satisfaction

- Inspiration

- Hope

- Optimism

- Psychological Resilience

- Psychological Health

The results provided strong correlation between positive emotions with the higher levels of the above scales. Negative emotions correlated with lower levels of the above scales. These observations supported the three broader functions of positive emotions that were theorized by other scientists in the late 1990s.

As a side note, hypothesis and theories in any science will eventually get tested for their validity once the measurement tools and testing methodology become available. I will repeat myself by saying that as a modern and independent field, psychology is only about 130 years old. In the time preceding, many psychological theories have been developed and clinically applied. Yet, not all of them have been proven through scientific methods. Whether or not scientific evidence is important when discussing emotions is up to you to decide.

In the beginning of the chapter, we saw how animals and humans use facial muscles to express various emotions. Numerous experiments have proven the theory that a deliberate facial expression can generate an emotion it expresses. Therefore, as I have already suggested in Chapter Six, deliberate smiling will tend to make us feel better. Try to experiment with other facial expression of other ways of expressing various types of emotions to see if you get to experience the emotion itself.

If part of our communication involves communicating our emotions by the virtue of body language, should we be conscious about what message we are actually sending? Is this message consistent with our verbal message? Which one do we recognize as more genuine? These questions come from the fact that the majority of communications between individuals are non-verbal. Some say it is 75%, while others insist on 93%. The "correct" number is irrelevant. What's important is our own awareness of facial expressions, posture, gestures, and the tone of voice that go along with words.

Emotional Intelligence.

When talking about roles and functions of emotions, the subject of Emotional Intelligence (EI) is important due to its proliferation. The term first was used in 1964, but it was not until the 1995 book by the same title that the term and the concept became popular.

EI is commonly defined as an ability to recognize our own emotions, emotions of others, discern between them, and use that knowledge in thinking and behavior. Alternatively, EI is the ability to incorporate information provided in non-verbal communication into verbal communication. There are several models of EI. They are: ability model, mixed model, and trait model. The ability model focuses on understanding emotions, the mixed model focuses on emotional skills, and the trait model concerns itself with self-perception. What one thinks about one's ability becomes one's ability. Some of you may have heard an expression: "You are not what you think you are, but what you think, you are." It describes the essence of the trait model.

Daniel Goleman, the author of *Emotional Intelligence,* also wrote *Working with Emotional Intelligence.* This 1998 book applies the mixed model to the workplace. Based on Goleman's research that includes surveys provided by hundreds of companies as well as interviews of executives, emotional intelligence is no less important than IQ in predicting one's professional success. The three must-have competencies for organization leadership are cognitive abilities measured by IQ, technical expertise, and emotional intelligence measured by EQ. The first two abilities are more important for entry-level job. However, the higher up the career ladder one climbs, the more important the EQ becomes. Goleman estimates that the emotional intelligence is twice more important than IQ and technical expertise combined. At the top level of the leadership, EQ is what differentiates successful leaders from the mediocre ones.

The emotional "smartness" (as I believe the word "intelligence" is used as being synonymous with "mastery," "ability," and "skills") within the mixed model is defined as having mastery over five key areas: self-awareness, self-regulation, motivation, empathy, and social skills. In *Working with Emotional Intelligence*, an emotional competence framework, as depicted in Figure 8.6, provides a great reference.[6]

Fig. 8.6

EMOTIONAL COMPETENCE FRAMEWORK

Personal Skills *(how we manage ourselves)*	**Self-awareness**	**Knowing one's internal states, preferences, resources, and intuitions**
	Emotional awareness	Recognizing one's emotions and their effects
	Accurate self-assessment	Knowing one's strengths and limits
	Self confidence	A strong sense of one's self-worth and capabilities
	Self-regulation	**Managing one's internal impulses and resources**
	Self-Control	Keeping disruptive emotions and impulses in check
	Trustworthiness	Maintaining standards of honesty and integrity
	Conscientiousness	Taking the resposibility for personal performance
	Adaptability	Flexibility in handling change
	Innovation	Being comfortable with novel ideas, approaches, and new information
	Motivation	**Emotional tendencies that guide or facilitate reaching goals**
	Achievement drive	Striving to improve or meet a standard of excellence
	Commitment	Aligning with goals of the group or organization
	Initiative	Readiness to act on opportunities
	Optimism	Persistence in pursuing goals despite obstacles and setbacks
Social Skills *(how we manage relationships)*	**Empathy**	**Awareness of other's feelings, needs, and concerns**
	Understanding others	Sensing others' feelings and perspectives, and taking active interest in their concerns
	Developing others	Sensing others' development needs and bolstering their abilities
	Service orientation	Anticipating, recognizing, and meeting customers' needs
	Leveraging diversity	Cultivating opportunities through different kinds of people
	Political awareness	Reading a group's emotional currents and power relationships
	Social Skills	**Adeptness and inducing desirable responses in others**
	Influence	Wielding effective tactics for persuasion
	Communication	Listening openly and sending convincing messages
	Conflict management	Negotiating and resolving disagreements
	Leadership	Inspiring and guiding individuals and groups
	Change catalyst	Initiating or managing change
	Building bonds	Nurturing instrumental relationships
	Collaboration & cooperation	Working with others toward shared goals
	Team capabilities	Creating group synergy in pursuing collective goals

To summarize, emotions, while confusing at times, are well-studied and are useful. They influence our behavior and communicate information to others through non-verbal means. Next, we turn our attention to feelings.

Feelings.

One of the ways to look at feelings is in terms of how they define relationships. Through regular communication we develop various relationships with people. We also develop certain feelings towards them. The ability to identify and to understand these feelings is certainly helpful in understanding the relationships.

As we have established before, emotions are shorter in their duration than feelings. Therefore, different emotions may come and go between two people as often as daily, while the feelings remain unchanged for much longer.

In the order from negative to positive, six feelings, examined through a relationship perspective is the focus of next paragraphs.

Envy.

Envy is typically defined as a strong desire to possess certain qualities, status, or material goods that other individuals or groups have. In experiencing envy, a person may also experience aggression towards an object of envy, wishing physical harm or even death. Envy is one of the seven deadly sins in Christianity. Other religions view envy as an emotional distraction.

To add to the complexity of this feeling, envy can either be malicious or benign. Benign envy motivates us to achieve goals that others have already achieved in a positive manner.

Envy is impossible without comparison. Only through comparison do we realize that other people may have material possessions, social status, or personal qualities that we want. Often, we discover new things that other people have that become objects of our desire. The difference between a simple desire and a malicious envy is that the latter takes a strong hold of our perspective on confidence, self-esteem, and happiness. Envy becomes a constant distraction and eats away at our hearts. It poisons and ruins many, if not most, relationships.

Overcoming envy is a difficult task. The good news is it can be done. Turning malicious envy into benign envy by trying to feel happy for the person is one approach. Additional strategies include practicing gratitude and developing an abundance mentality as opposed to a scarcity viewpoint. Focusing on personal goals, also known as "getting a life," is a great distraction from constantly comparing ourselves with others. Automatic comparison will always be a part of our psyche. It is through a conscious effort of rational thought that we can keep envy at bay.

Jealousy.

Sometimes envy and jealousy are used interchangeably, which is an error. This simple rule that will help to differentiate the terms is the number of parties involved. Envy is a feeling that is originated by one person towards possessions of another through comparison. Envy requires two parties. Unlike envy, jealousy requires three parties. First is a person with jealous feelings, the second person is on the receiving end, and the third person is a reason for the first person to experience jealousy. The third person may or may not exist in reality, but must exist in the mind of the first for jealousy to be trigger.

Jealousy is a complex feeling and encompasses several other feelings and emotions such as fear, insecurity, inadequacy, resentment, and anger. Depending on how real the threat to the relationship is, the actions towards the third person may vary from inaction to physical violence. The same may be true towards the second person. A great literary example of that is Shakespeare's story of Othello and Desdemona.

Unlike envy, jealousy is accepted in Western culture as a normal part of a closed relationship. The need to know whether a threat to a relationship is real or not is perceived as a legitimate reason to hire a private investigator.

Experts suggest women and men view jealousy through different lenses. For women, jealousy that is based on emotional attraction only creates far more fear of losing a partner than for men. However, both men and women react similarly to the physical infidelity of their respective partners.

When the threat of infidelity is a factor, the outcome will depend on many factors. However, if jealousy is just a feeling based on suspicion, it can ruin a relationship. There are ways to overcome jealousy. Some recommend distrusting the significance of the emotions that fuel jealousy, while others suggest working on self-confidence as a way to re-establish self-trust and a trust towards your partner. In my life, I have experienced a fair amount of jealousy and it taught me some extremely valuable lessons.

Aggression.

With or without provocation, a strong feeling with intent to cause harm to another individual would be a general definition of aggression. It can also be communicated verbally or non-verbally. Unlike envy or jealousy, aggression can be experienced in total isolation. Aggression can be a way to achieve a certain goal, or spark a reaction and cause some uncontrollable actions. The first type, in general, is more socially acceptable than the second. It all depends on a particular situation.

Aggression comes with certain benefits. It motivates competition for resources and when acted upon within moral and legal norms, aggression fuels progress. We can also observe aggressive behavior in sports. Yet, aggression as a steady feeling towards another human being, is destructive.

Similar to certain emotions, aggression is hardwired in our brain. In certain animals, the amygdala structure, when stimulated, results in more aggressive behavior. The prefrontal cortex, which is the most developed in humans, is a control mechanism that often counters the impulses coming from amygdala. The control comes from learning what behavior is acceptable and what is not. Nevertheless, there are situations when we simply lose control, or choose not to exercise it.

The biology of aggression centered on testosterone as a causal hormone with serotonin keeping aggression in check. I was surprised to learn that oxytocin, also referred as a "hugging hormone" or "love hormone" leads to violence. Many studies point to oxytocin as a cause hormone of aggression when protecting offspring or a love partner. High levels of cortisol, a "stress hormone," and adrenaline may also lead to aggression.

There are many tools to self-manage aggression as well as several aggression management models that help prevent violence in workplace. Both require a combination of subject matter education, knowing what to look for, and best practices on how to manage conflicts.

Attachment.

Applicable mostly to the years of early development, attachment creates a strong bond between two people, a child and a mother, for instance. If you are interested in this topic, I would recommend to look into works of John Bowlby. His most significant contribution to the field is the trilogy that consists of *Attachment* (1969), *Anxiety and Anger* (1972), and *Loss:*

Sadness and Depression (1980). However, attachment is experienced by adults as well. According to Hazan and Shaver (1987), some of the features that transfer from an attachment relationship between an infant and a caregiver to a romantic (attachment) relationship between two adults are: [7]

- Both feel safe when the other is nearby and responsiveBoth engage in close, intimate, bodily contact

- Both feel insecure when the other is inaccessible

- Both share discoveries with one another

- Both exhibit fascination and preoccupation with one another

- Both engage in "baby talk"

Let's dwell on the above for a moment. Do you recognize any of these in your current relationships? While for some the word "attachment" may connote with "dependency," I believe that a romantic relationship that is based on attachment is full of trust toward the "caregiver." If so, what other characteristics of the relationship can trust lead to? What are some other long-term feelings rooted in trust?

Friendship.

The foundation of friendship between adults is based on a mutual attraction, unlike love, for instance. Argyle and Henderson, the experts in the area of friendship, state the following basis for it:[8]

- Material and informational support

- Social support (i.e. advice, empathy, sharing of secrets)

- Common interests and activities

Argyle's data shows that women are more inclined to share intimate details with their female friends, while men are more likely to work and play together as an expression of their friendship. Friendship between men and women can show in a variety of forms.

How do we choose friends? Just how much do we have to have in common with another person to create a strong bond? Both field studies and general recommendations point to the fact that we choose based on commonality in values and goals. We tend to gravitate to those that can help us learn new things. Personal traits of friends may vary from very similar to completely different.[9]

Friendship has its rules. Typically, they include sharing news, good or bad; emotional support; and helping each other at the time of need. Also, it is expected between friends to repay favors or monetary obligations. When it comes to representation, one friend is expected to protect the image of another and to remain polite towards other friends. What are some other rules you have among your friends? Regular violations of these rules may lead to friendship dissolution. Additional reasons for the friendship to end include changes in one or both individual's geographic location and lifestyle. Finally, changes in the emotional content of the friendship plays a crucial role in either strengthening or weakening the bond. If the relationship is more and more characterized by defensiveness, stonewalling, criticism, and disrespect, the probability of dissolution will increase.

Take a moment to think about someone who you consider to be a close friend. How did the friendship start? What types of challenges did it encounter along the way? What have you learned about yourself as the result of overcoming the challenges?

Love.

We use word love to describe a large variety of positive feelings and emotions. Love and like are often used interchangeably. Both may be used to express a strong attraction towards goods, services, ideas or even food and drink. When we really like something, we may say "I love it!" Also, we say "I love my job" and "I love my country!" We experience a different kind of love towards nature and wildlife as we may establish a closer connection with living species. The relationship with our pets can be similar to that of a family member. That will manifest with even stronger feelings. That said, love as a feeling that describes a relationship between two individuals is the focus of this discussion. Figure 8.7 provides a quick reference on different forms of love. Based on triangular theory of love, developed by Robert Sternberg, the three components of love are passion, intimacy, and commitment.

Fig. 8.7

	Intimacy	Passion	Commitment
Non Love	-	-	-
Liking	+	-	-
Infatuated Love	-	+	-
Empty Love	-	-	+
Romantic Love	+	+	-
Companionate Love	+	-	+
Fatuous Love	-	+	+
Consumate Love	+	+	+

Inclusion or exclusion of the three components in the relationship will determine the form of love. The same table could be graphically represented as overlapping circles. (Fig 8.8)

Fig. 8.8

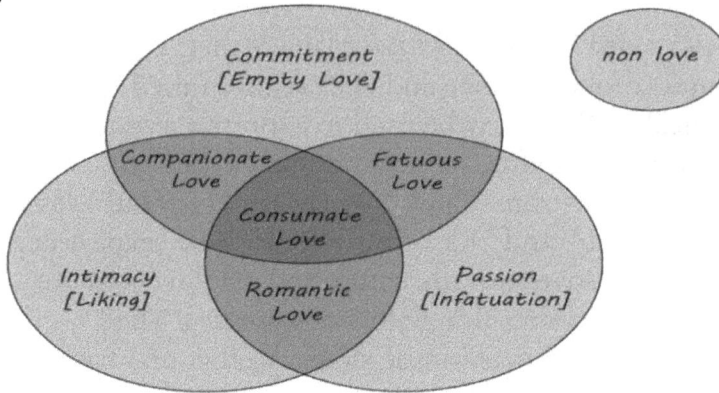

Items in [ ] indicate type of love when other components are absent.
A relationship without any of the 3 components is non love.

- Non love is included in the theory as a term that means an absence of any intimacy, passion, or commitment.

- Liking, infatuation, and empty love are single forms of love that are based on either intimacy, or passion, or commitment, respectively.

- Romantic love, while passionate and intimate, has no commitment.

- Love that is intimate and with the element of commitment is called companionate. However, this love is without a passion. Often, this type of relationship is seen in long-term marriages.

- "Love at the first sight" is a great example of fatuous love where passion and commitment comes to the forefront, leaving out intimacy.

- Consummate love has all the components. Couples that have achieved that kind of relationship are often called "perfect." This is more of a theoretical construct: in reality, the relationship may as any of the above and a couple may strive towards achieving and maintaining all the components.

Take a few moments to reflect on the relationship you may have with a significant other. Where does it fall within the framework of the theory? Do you agree?

**

Throughout this book I have presented many theories and you do not have to necessarily agree with them. You don't have to take into consideration any of the scientific evidence from the previous chapters either. However, if you have found something that sparked your interest, try it.

***

Chapter Summary.

The Four Wheel Alignment Model, as described in chapters one through seven, had a few hits regarding the role of feelings and emotions, but lacked a deeper dive. That was done in an attempt to keep the Model relatively simple to comprehend. Making things difficult or confusing hardly encourages any action. At the same time, a book that claims to help individuals achieve a life of harmony must allocate an adequate space and thought for emotional subject matter.

Getting clarity around our feelings and emotions can be a daunting task: there are thousands of words that describe how we feel. With all this linguistic abundance, there are a few dozen words that come from other languages and do not translate to English directly!

Talking about feelings and emotions as a part of the metaphoric Model, I have compared them to air inside the tires. Indeed, every driving situation requires an optimal amount of air. Yet, before we can manage feelings and emotions, we need to understand their nature and purpose. That's where some research is appropriate.

The proposed framework of the chapter separates feelings from emotions based mostly on the longevity of respective experiences. Discussion of emotions was purposely tied to recent scientific discoveries, while feelings were viewed using the relationship perspective. This approach was only effective if you gained an ounce of help. Did you? Let me know.

Endnotes

Chapter One

1. Doran, G. T. (Nov. 1981). There's a S.M.A.R.T. way to write management's goals and objectives. *Management Review*. 70.11

Chapter Two

1. Smith, G. (March 14, 2012). Why am I Leaving Goldman Sachs. *The New York Times*. P A27

2. Guiso, L., Sapienza, P., & Zingales, L. (2013). The Value of Corporate Culture. National Bureau of Economic Research. Cambridge, MA.

3. Plank Center for Leadership in Public Relations. (n.d.). Retrieved on September 10, 2016 from https://www.bulldogreporter.com/pr-industry-leadership-crisis-new-plank-center-report-reveals-wide-ga/

4. Kaygin, E., Gulluce, A. C. (February 2013). The Relationship between Career Choice and Individual Vales: A Case Study of a Turkish University. *International Journal of Humanities and Social Science*. 3 (3)

5. U.S. Census Bureau (2015). Retrieved from https://www.bls.gov/oes/current/oes419022.htm; https://www.bls.gov/oes/current/oes151134.htm; https://www.bls.gov/oes/current/oes532012.htm

6. Life Coach Spotter. (n.d.). Retrieved on September 22, 2016 from http://www.lifecoachspotter.com/what-is-your-purpose-in-life/

Chapter Three

1. United States v. Clark, 360 F. Supp. 936 (S.D.N.Y 1973).

2. Katzenbach, J. R., Steffen, I., & Kronley, C. (August 2012).

Cultural Change That Sticks. *Harvard Business Review.*

3. Unicef. (n.d.). Retrieved on September 28, 2016 from http://www.unicef.org/crc/files/Rights_overview.pdf

4. Blair, R., Lutterbie, R. (Spring 2011). Introduction: Journal of Dramatic theory and criticism's special section on cognitive studies, theatre, and performance. *Journal of Dramatic theory and criticism.*

5. Lewis, M. M. (1989). Liar's Poker: Rising Through the Wreckage on Wall Street. New York. W.W. Norton & Company.

Chapter Four

1. Harper, J. (1972). Slaves and Freemen in Imperial Rome. *American Journal of Physiology.*

2. Van Zanden, Jan Luiten, *et al.* (2014), "Global Well-being since 1820", in Jan Luiten, *et al.* (eds.), How Was Life?: Global Well-being since 1820, OECD Publishing.

3. Retrieved from https://knoema.com/nwnfkne/world-gdp-ranking-2016-data-and-charts-forecast; https://en.wikipedia.org/wiki/List_of_countries_by_GDP_(PPP)_per_capita.; http://worldhappiness.report/wp-content/uploads/sites/2/2016/03/HR-V1_web.pdf.

4. Stiglitz, J. (n.d.). Retrieved on October 6, 2016 from https://www.weforum.org/agenda/2016/04/beyond-gdp-is-it-time-to-rethink-the-way-we-measure-growth/

5. Zubrick, S. R., Williams, A. A., & Silburn, S.R. (May 2000) Indicators of Social and Family Functioning. Department of Family and Community Services.

6. Komocsin, L. (2012). Toolful Coach. SPARKLE Coaching Model with 150 Useful Tools and Case Studies. pp 97-99.

Chapter Five

1. Klaus, P. (2011). Customer Experience: Are We Measuring Right Things? *International Journal of Market Research*, 53 (6) *pp. 771-792.*

2. Freeston, M. H., Rhéaume, J., Letarte, H., Dugas, M. J., & Ladouceur, R. (1994). Why do people worry? *Personality and Individual Differences*, 17, pp 791–802.

3. Technique. Author Unknown. (n.d.). Retrieved from https://www.getselfhelp.co.uk/worrytree.htm

4. Ordonez, L. D., Schweitzer, M.E., Galinsky, A.D, & Bazerman, M.H. (2009). Goals Gone Wild: The Systematic Side Effects of Over-Prescribing Goal Setting. Harvard Business School.

Chapter Six

1. Scheier, M.F., Carver, C. S., (1985). Optimism, Coping, and Health: Assessment and Implications of Generalized Outcome Expectancies. *Health Psychology*, 4 (3) pp 219-247.

2. Villarica, H. (April 2012). How the Power of Positive Thinking Won Scientific Credibility. *The Atlantic.*

3. David R. Hawkins, M.D. (2013). Power vs. Force. The Hidden Determinants of Human Behavior. Carlsbad, CA. Hay House. pp 90-91.

Chapter Seven

1. McManus, C. (2002). Right hand left hand. The origins of asymmetry in brain, bodies, atoms, and cultures. Harvard University Press. p. 183.

2. Midlife crisis. In *Merriam-webster.com*. Retrieved from https://www.merriam-

webster.com/dictionary/midlife%20crisis

3. Midlife. In *Thefreedictionary.com*. Retrieved from
http://www.thefreedictionary.com/midlife

4. Crisis. In *Merriam-webster.com*. Retrieved from
https://www.merriam-webster.com/dictionary/crisis

5. National Institute of Aging. (1995-1996) Retrieved from
http://www.midus.wisc.edu/scopeofstudy.php

6. Loftus, E. (2013) How reliable is your memory? [TED]
Retrieved from
https://www.ted.com/talks/elizabeth_loftus_the_fiction_of_m
emory

7. Beyerstein, B., Beyerstein, D. (1992). The Write Stuff.
Evaluations of Graphology - The Study of Handwriting
Analysis. Amherst, NY. Prometheus Books.

8. Forer, B.R. (1949). The fallacy of personal validation: A
classroom demonstration of gullibility. *Journal of Abnormal and
Social Psychology*. American Psychological Association. 44 (1) pp
118-123.

9. Kaheman, D., Deaton, A. (2010). High income improves
evaluation of life but do not emotional well-being. Center for
Health and Well-being, Princeton University.

10. Diener, E., Silegman, M. (2004). Beyond Money. Toward an
Economy of Well-Being. *Psychology*. 5 (1). p. 10.

11. Diener, E., Silegman, M. (2004). Beyond Money. Toward an
Economy of Well-Being. *Psychology*. 5 (1). p.13.

12. The General Social Survey. (n.d.). National Opinion
Research Center. University of Chicago. Retrieved on February
24, 2017 from
https://dalrock.wordpress.com/2011/06/25/does-divorce-

make-people-happy/

Chapter Eight

1. Berridge, K. C., Kringelbach, M.L. (2015). Pleasure Systems in the Brain. *Neuron.* 44 (3). pp 646-664.

2. Orthony, A., Turner, T.J. (1990). What's basic about basic emotions? *Pschychological Review.* 97(3). pp 315-331.

3. Panksepp, J. (2000). The neuro-evolutionary cusp between emotions and cognitions: Implications for understanding consciousness and the emergence of a unified mind science *Consciousness & Emotion.* 1(1). pp 15-54.

4. Izard, C.E, Ackerman, B.P. (2000). Motivational, Organizational, and Regulatory Functions of Discrete Emotions. In Lewis, M., Haviland-Jones, J.M., (Ed.) Handbook of Emotions, Second Edition. pp 253-260. Guilford Publications, Inc. New York.

5. Galanakis, M., Stalikas, A., Pezirkiandis, C., & Karakasidou, I (2016). Reliability and Validity of the Modified Differential Emotions Slace (mDES) in a Greek Sample. *Pshychology,* (7). pp 101-113.

6. Goleman, D. (1998). Working with Emotional Intelligence. New York. Bantam Dell. pp 26-27.

7. Hazan, C., Shaver, P. (1987). Romantic love conceptualized as an attachment process. Journal of Personality and Social Psychology, (52). pp 511-524.

8. Argyle M., Henderson M. (1984). The rules of friendship. *Journal of Social and Personal Relationship.* 1 (2). pp 211-237.

9. Kandel D.B., (1978). Similarity in real-life adolescent friendship pairs. *Journal of Social and Personal Relationship.* 1. pp 306-312.

About the Author

Dmitry Kondratyev was born in 1970 in Moscow, but until the age of twelve resided in Yakutsk, near Oymakon, Russia, the coldest place on Earth. Upon his family's return to Moscow and high school graduation, Dmitry pursued his first bachelor's degree in music history.

In 1989, Dmitry and his family left the Soviet Union and on Valentine's Day in 1990 they arrived to Ann Arbor, Michigan. Before graduating from the University of Michigan in 1996 and starting his banking career in 1997, Dmitry tried seventeen jobs in six industries. He refers to that time as his "getting to know America" phase. In 2004, Dmitry graduated from Oakland University with a MBA in Finance.

In the last ten years of his banking career, Dmitry helped hundreds of small business owners. Paying close attention to their decision making processes as well as to how these decisions affected not just their business, but their lives, Dmitry became naturally drawn to coaching.

Today, Dmitry Kondratyev is a Certified Professional Coach and holds Associate Certified Coach credentials issued by the International Coach Federation. Dmitry is also a board member of the Michigan Chapter of the ICF. He enjoys coaching professionals and small business owners and continues to provide commercial lending solutions as a Vice President at Main Street Bank.

Dmitry with his wife Olga and two children, Katherine and Jacob, reside in Troy, Michigan.

Contact Dmitry at dmitry@positivecoachingllc.com

www.ingramcontent.com/pod-product-compliance
Lightning Source LLC
Chambersburg PA
CBHW070036100426
42740CB00013B/2702